# Additional Praise for *At the Heart of Work*

"Implementing the 6 Levers Framework has empowered us to intentionally develop systems that align with and strengthen our culture, propelling our mission forward and enabling us to achieve our goals with remarkable speed. This book is an essential guide for anyone seeking to achieve similar success"

— **KATRINA CAMPBELL, CEO, BRIGHTON CENTER**

"This book is both empowering and humbling in its guidance. It is a necessary and practical companion to any team that wants to work with intention instead of just reacting. By following the 6 Levers framework, my team and I grew as leaders, listeners, problem solvers and strategic thinkers, together."

— **EVITA MORIN, CEO, RISE RECOVERY**

"Leadership is no longer merely a noun in today's dynamic post-COVID era, but rather an action verb filled with new disciplines once thought aspirational of leaders. At The Heart of Work identifies many of these critical leadership traits and has helped my leadership team focus on the constant behaviors necessary to deliver continuous success while fueling a healthy culture."

— **ANDRIE LEDAY, GLOBAL MEDTECH EXECUTIVE AND 2019 GLOBAL INNOVATIONS FELLOW**

"At the Heart of Work" gets to the root of the challenges that often hold back well-intentioned organizations. The 6 Levers Framework seamlessly connects values, culture, and everyday practices, offering a clear path to meaningful transformation. This is a must-read for leaders who seek to elevate organizational performance through core, sustainable practices—rather than chasing the next new initiative."

— **ALISTAIR DEAKIN, CEO, SIGBEE AND TURNAROUND SPECIALIST**

"Every business is in the people system. The word "company" comes from an Italian word for 2 people having bread together and the root of "Organization" is "organism," so there's more people and biology than there is mechanics and structure to business success. No operating system will accomplish vitality if it's not deliberately people-encompassing, and the 6 Levers framework will invite you to address the systemic rhythms for success as a human leading humans!"

— **MIKE SHARROW, CEO, C-12**

"At the Heart of Work is an essential guide for leaders at every level. This book empowers leaders with practical strategies to transform team challenges into opportunities for growth, helping them emerge stronger and more resilient."

— **JESSICA LOMBARD, DIRECTOR OF LEARNING AND DEVELOPMENT, SAN ANTONIO AREA FOUNDATION**

"Strategy outlines your vision; a system brings it to life. Integrating the 6 Levers framework into my consulting practice has been transformative, providing me with a versatile and adaptable set of tools to build intentional and practical systems that resonate with business leaders across all types of industries. This framework empowers my clients to drive meaningful impact and execute their vision with clarity and purpose, while also giving them the tools needed to build a healthy culture."

— **PHILLIP HERNANDEZ, FOUNDER AND CEO, MISSION MENTOR CONSULTING AND 6 LEVERS COACH**

"Any business book that purports to be "with and for people" in its approach to leading an organization resonates with me. Using lots of stories and examples, At the Heart of Work (ATHOW) captures the essence of leading an organization well, while providing tons of practical steps for taking action. I particularly liked the chapter on "Cohesion" with its emphasis on collaboration among teams, including the use of an orchestra as a metaphor, which happens to be my favorite. ATHOW provides a clear and compelling framework for designing work that is both impactful and meaningful."

— **MARK MCCLAIN, CEO AND FOUNDER OF SAILPOINT TECHNOLOGIES AND AUTHOR OF "JOY AND SUCCESS AT WORK: BUILDING ORGANIZATIONS THAT DON'T SUCK (THE LIFE OUT OF PEOPLE)"**

"The 6 Levers framework has been one the best tools for me to build culture within our diverse and young team. It has helped us double in size and win second best place to work in our city. Getting to the heart of work is what our company strives for. It inspires our people at every level of the company and helps its leaders attack the root cause of issues. It has been the fuel we use to accomplish our mission."

— **CHARLES WOODIN, CEO, GEEKDOM**

"The 6 Levers framework has been transformative for our organization. It's helped us craft a comprehensive strategic plan and provided a clear path to success and the tools to execute it. The results have been exceptional. From 2021 to 2025, our annual revenue increased by 150%, growing from $24.9 million to a projected $62.3 million while our workforce expanded by nearly 95%, growing from 577 employees to over 1,000. The insights from At the Heart of Work have been pivotal, equipping us with the clarity and framework to navigate challenges with speed, flexibility, and precision, enabling us to achieve our goals."

— **RON EKSTRAND, CEO, EASTERSEALS ARKANSAS**

*preparing lessons, grading assessments, and striving to create the best learning environment possible. My passion and dedication were fueled by the connections I made with my students, the rigor and autonomy I found in my role, and the contribution I felt I was making as part of a broader school community. Leading a classroom and stewarding my students' learning was incredibly fulfilling and made the hard work worthwhile. We had fun, and together, we achieved remarkable results. By the end of the year, my students were outperforming nearly every school in the district. Some of the best years of my life were those I spent teaching, and the impact of my experience in that role and in those schools will last a lifetime. It was looking back on this experience years later that taught me a core idea of our book: when our work is meaningful, we become deeply engaged, productive, and even more effective.*

— Joe

◆ ◆ ◆

*In the immediate aftermath of Hurricane Katrina, people drove up I-55 all the way to the Midwest. Thousands stopped in St. Louis, seeking support. Many nonprofits responded to the need, and the organization I worked for, St. Patrick Center, was one of them. We formed a group of five leaders from diverse backgrounds and professions, and I was asked to lead this newly formed team.*

*I had never been more energized. Although this wasn't my first time leading a team, it was my first time doing so without a playbook to follow. However, I had something far more valuable than a playbook: I was given autonomy and a great sense of trust to solve each new problem that came our way. On the surface, you might think, "Sure, who wouldn't find meaning in helping people experiencing homelessness find new homes?" Well, I wasn't that happy in my role before I was offered this opportunity. In fact, I was considering leaving. Even though I loved the mission itself, when I was given autonomy and a way to make a meaningful contribution, I was more engaged than I had ever been.*

*The results of our efforts surpassed all my expectations. By the first anniversary of Hurricane Katrina, our team had raised $3 million in support and successfully relocated 325 families into permanent housing in St. Louis. As amazing as it was to find new homes for 325 families, the accomplishment I was most proud of was identifying and training 325 community groups to adopt each family and provide ongoing support. These community groups included churches, HOAs, cycling clubs, and more. It was truly awe-inspiring to see so many people in our community answer the call.*

— Shaun

◆ ◆ ◆

*When I landed my first job out of college at World Wide Technology (WWT), I found myself immersed in an environment unlike any I had experienced before. WWT, a multibillion-dollar organization, was renowned not only for its success but also for its culture. As someone who had always been part of sports teams through college, I initially thought I understood team dynamics. However, what I witnessed at WWT was a methodical and intentional approach to communicating, promoting, and implementing values across a massive organization. During my time at WWT, I saw firsthand the power of a strong, value-driven culture. This experience ignited a desire in me to one day create a similar environment.*

*Despite my love of the work and culture at WWT, I knew I needed to pursue a different career route. That's when my dad and I started Mission Matters*

# Contents

Preface ............................................... 6

People and Systems ................................. 15

The 6 Levers Framework ............................ 31

Identity ............................................. 51

Leadership .......................................... 77

Focus ............................................... 105

Rhythm .............................................. 125

Cohesion ............................................ 153

Momentum ........................................... 179

Getting Started ..................................... 199

It's a Journey ...................................... 213

Notes ............................................... 218

# Preface

Do you find meaning in your work? For many, the answer is no.

A McKinsey & Company report from 2021 found that 70% of respondents are looking for a sense of purpose in their work. A related question asked how many people actually found purpose in their work, and the results were staggering. A whopping 86% of executives said they did, but only 15% of frontline managers and employees said the same. We wrote this book because we believe it's possible for more than just the few at the top to find joy and purpose in their work.

◆ ◆ ◆

*My first job out of college was teaching seventh-grade math at Martin Luther King Jr. Middle School in Charlotte, North Carolina. Despite being young, inexperienced, and not from the community, I was committed to building a classroom culture where students could thrive. One of my most vivid memories from that time is driving to school each morning in the dark, arriving just before 6:00 a.m., when I knew our head custodian would be there to open the door with a smile. With a generous cup of coffee at my side, I'd dive into final lesson preparation, making tweaks to specific exercises and reviewing class rosters and student data to ensure I had the right support in place. In these moments, I found myself in a certain state of flow, fully engaged and confident that my efforts would make a significant contribution.*

*I showed up before sunrise not because I had to but because the work was incredibly meaningful to me. I spent early mornings and late evenings*

RETHINKING WHAT IT TAKES TO BUILD A HEALTHY
ORGANIZATION WITH THE 6 LEVERS FRAMEWORK

# AT THE HEART
# *of* WORK

**SHAUN LEE**  **JOE OLWIG**

WITH JOSHUA ARANDA

**THE SELF PUBLISHING AGENCY**

Shaun Lee, Joe Olwig, Josh Aranda
At the Heart of Work
*Rethinking What it Takes to Build a Healthy Organization with the 6 Levers Framework*

TSPA The Self Publishing Agency, Inc.
Copyright © 2024 by Shaun Lee, Joe Olwig, Josh Aranda
First Edition

Hardcover ISBN 978-1-954233-41-6
Softcover ISBN 978-1-954233-40-9
eBook ISBN 978-1-954233-42-3

All rights reserved under International and Pan-American Copyright Conventions. Manufactured in the United States of America.

No part of this publication may be reproduced, stored in, or introduced into a retrieval system, transmitted in any form or by any means (electronic, mechanical, photocopying, recording, or otherwise), and/or otherwise used in any manner for purposes of training artificial intelligence technologies to generate text, including, without limitation, technologies that are capable of generating works in the same style or genre as this publication, without the prior written permission of the publisher.

This book is sold subject to the condition that it shall not, by way of trade or otherwise, be lent, resold, hired out, or otherwise circulated without the publisher's prior written consent in any form of binding, cover, or condition other than that in which it was published.

Contributing Author | Christie Albrecht
Book Design | Angela Campbell
Front Cover Illustration | Ellen Wolbert
Graphic & Illustration Design | Tracy Hetherington
Editor | Jennifer Jas
Publishing Management | TSPA The Self Publishing Agency, Inc.

*Group. Inspired by the rigor and discipline I had observed at WWT, I aimed to replicate that level of commitment to culture while delivering outstanding results. However, I soon realized that achieving this was much easier said than done. The leaders at WWT made it look effortless because they operated within a cohesive system that was understood by all. This system encompassed everything from how they ran meetings to how they cultivated leadership at all levels and to how they planned on a quarterly basis. It was a model of focus and intentionality.*

*My time there still informs why I pursue meaningful work and aim to create healthy environments. It also planted a seed for helping me to understand the intersection of systems and people. When we get a taste of meaningful work, it engages us deeply, which makes us more productive and enhances our lives overall.*

*We chose to write this book because we wanted to make it easier for anyone to understand how to intentionally build more purposeful ways of working.*

— Joshua

◆ ◆ ◆

Roles like the ones mentioned in our stories had a huge impact on our lives and well-being. We have also seen the impact on the hundreds of clients we have worked with over the last decade-plus. The problem is that, all too often, these seasons don't last. It's fleeting and difficult to sustain, but we don't believe it has to be this way.

We are Joe, Josh, and Shaun, and we created the 6 Levers framework out of a passion to equip teams with the practical tools and resources needed to build organizational health that lasts. We come from different backgrounds and a mix of experiences ranging from technology to education, nonprofits to start-ups, and social work to sustainable food businesses. What brought us together is that we want every person to find meaning and purpose in their work. We want every worker to have the opportunity to experience work that is meaningful, life-giving, and joyful. Not once or twice or every now and then, but most of the time. We want to make it possible for any team to begin building healthier ways of working.

We developed the 6 Levers framework based on several core beliefs about the workplace, driven by our concern for many of the leaders and teams we've worked with who view their workplaces as sources of stress and frustration. This frustration often stems not from a lack of effort or investment but from an inability to access the necessary systems to build the desired work culture. In empathizing with these challenges, we developed the foundational beliefs for 6 Levers. These beliefs are the cornerstone of our identity and serve as our guiding principles as we continue to evolve and refine the 6 Levers framework. They are our north star as we continue to develop 6 Levers.

### Our Beliefs

Everyone can find purpose and meaning in their work.

We need to design systems that center human needs.

Inclusively designed systems increase engagement and organizational resiliency.

Organizational health is more than a means to an end.

## We believe everyone can find purpose and meaning in their work.

Our work is an important part of our identity as humans and our sense of purpose in life. When we see our work as more than just a job and feel we are contributing to a larger purpose, we are more motivated, engaged, and committed. This intrinsic motivation drives personal growth and satisfaction and creates a sense of belonging and shared purpose within a team. We are better equipped to overcome challenges, stay focused on shared goals, and contribute to the health and success of the organization.

## We believe we need to design systems that center human needs.

Our work systems are powered by people, and we believe that in order to build a healthy organization, we must keep fundamental human needs at the center of what we do. Those needs include a sense of meaning, belonging, contribution, and clarity, to name a few. When our systems center these needs, we are more likely to create the conditions in which employees are truly engaged in their work and environments where employees feel valued and connected to each other and the broader mission. This sense of belonging nurtures collaboration and a shared sense of purpose, which are essential for team cohesion and productivity. When employees have clarity about their roles and priorities, it reduces ambiguity and stress, allowing them to focus on their tasks more effectively.

## We believe that inclusively designed systems increase engagement and resiliency.

Systems work better and organizations are healthier when people are involved in designing how work works within their teams. This inclusion makes team members more engaged and resilient. Teams feel a greater sense of ownership over the work and the results when they collaboratively design their ways of working. This meets their needs for autonomy and empowerment. When people feel that their voices are heard and their ideas are valued in the design process, they become more engaged as they see their direct impact on the team's operations. They are more likely to adapt to change because they have a deeper understanding of the system's flexibility and how it can evolve to address new challenges.

## We believe organizational health is more than a means to an end.

An organization that prioritizes its health creates a dynamic, connected, and life-giving culture. This, in turn, leads to greater employee satisfaction, reduced turnover, improved teamwork, and increased resilience in the face of challenges. In addition, pursuing organizational health has benefits that expand far beyond the impact on the organization. A healthier work culture means that the people working in it are much more likely to positively impact their circles of influence outside of work as well. Rather than being drained and only offering the little that remains, they are energized to offer the best parts of themselves. Pursuing organizational health as a distinct goal creates a more fulfilling and meaningful journey for all involved—and even those who aren't.

# How to Read This Book

Our goal is to provide you with an understanding of the foundations of the 6 Levers framework and to give you a series of tools and concepts you can begin applying with your team.

You can read this book in a couple of ways:

1. Start to finish
2. Start with the first two chapters, then choose a Lever that most resonates with you and move there

The 6 Levers framework is designed to be modular and flexible. We recognize that different teams have different needs, and if you have one particular concern that is top of mind, feel free to start with that chapter.

In each Lever chapter, you will find tools and new approaches that you can put into practice right away. The last two chapters will give you ideas on how to get started implementing the 6 Levers in your organization. If you want to go deeper, visit www.6levers.co to learn more.

# People and Systems

We've worked with hundreds of organizations over the past decade in pursuit of building healthier workplaces, and we've seen a common pattern. When leaders are faced with a challenge—low team performance, unresolved conflict, or employee disengagement—their default diagnosis of the issue is almost always that people are the source of the problem. It sounds like this:

- John's not a culture fit.
- I don't think Erika has what it takes.
- People don't like change. Every time I try something new, I get pushback.
- Sarah and Marcus don't get along. Their personalities keep clashing.
- Grace gets overwhelmed easily. It's a fast-paced work environment, but everyone else manages fine.
- When I give the team a chance to share input, I hear crickets.

These may look like people issues—after all, each scenario involves people—but a closer examination often uncovers a far more complex set of factors affecting our teams and leading to tension or low performance. A deeper look often reveals an entire host of "'non-people'" issues. From cultural norms that promote the wrong behaviors and organizational structures that fail to meet employee needs to ineffective processes and inefficient workflows, the root of our issues as leaders extends far beyond the decisions and capabilities of the people involved.

Imagine a school where the administration is frustrated by underperforming teachers. Their immediate assumption? "We've got to find better teachers." But in reality, the teachers are burned out as they often face an inflexible work environment, unattractive pay, and an unrealistic set of demands when it comes to effectively leading their classrooms every day.

In a fulfillment center, the head of manufacturing is vexed by high packing error rates and wonders, "Why can't we find line supervisors with better attention to detail?" Meanwhile, staffing levels have remained stagnant despite a 20% increase in volume, and line supervisors are frustrated that management hands down new procedures without any input from the team on the ground.

In a technology product company, the founder and CEO is frustrated with Mark, the leader of the product development team. Customer feedback has made it clear which features to focus on in the product roadmap, and in her mind, the CEO has aligned with Mark on these priorities. At the peak of her frustration, she tells a few other members of the executive team, "I'm just not sure Mark is the right person. We've been clear about the features to prioritize, yet he can't seem to bring the level of focus and discipline that this team needs." Meanwhile, the reality for Mark is that two other members of the executive team have been lobbying for feature changes regularly, and the process for feature prioritization has been anything but collaborative. Mark has felt torn as he wants to be responsive to all members of the executive team. Underneath this tension between Mark and his CEO lies issues with role clarity, leader autonomy, prioritization practices, and the Executive Team's weekly meeting—each of which contributes to lower performance and declining team cohesion.

Looking at each situation, we must expand our analysis of the issue beyond the performance of individual workers. We must also consider the impact of the existing norms, processes, and structures that influence the behaviors and actions of employees. The performance of an individual worker or the interpersonal tension inside a team is often a signal of a deeper issue. These challenges are rarely as straightforward as "John not being a culture fit." More often, the conditions defining John's workplace have failed to adequately support his success. We often assume—incorrectly—that the person or people involved in the issue are chiefly responsible. But more often than not, the events or outcomes that we as leaders label as "'issues'" stem from a gap in the underlying systems.

# Why Leaders Miss the Mark

As leaders, we can get better at diagnosing these issues. If we regularly misdiagnose what's going on, we end up solving the wrong problems. First, we need to understand the forces that have contributed to our current workplace conditions—forces that make it hard to regularly and accurately understand the source of our most challenging problems.

## It's Easier to Blame People

When we start working with a new organization, it usually only takes a couple of weeks before someone mentions "the bus."

"It's been a real challenge for us. We have to get the right people on the bus, you know?" a leader might say.

It's a reference to the book *Good to Great: Why Some Companies Make the Leap ... And Others Don't.* Jim Collins speaks to the importance of getting the right people on the bus, the wrong people off the bus, and the right people in the right seats. When a leader starts talking about buses and seats, they are often experiencing a repeating performance issue where they're diagnosing the problem as someone simply being in the wrong role (it's a people issue, right?). Our default is to blame the person at the center of the performance issue.

Perhaps the most common reason we do this is that it's easier. Isolating a big problem to one person makes it feel solvable. Evaluating a group of people or a system is much more challenging and requires space that leaders often feel they don't have. Sometimes, the solution to a problem is to move someone off the bus or to a different seat, but we create problems when we don't look *beyond* these role issues. Don't get us wrong; we are grateful for Jim Collins's efforts to help teams consider "people fit" as a cause of our most challenging organizational issues. However, if we use this as the only criteria for understanding the source of the problem, we risk missing the deeper issues at play.

Immediately assuming people are the source of the problem is also a form of attribution bias. We tend to over-index for someone's personality or character without examining the situation they work in, and it causes us to assume the individual is the source of the problem. We tell ourselves, "If we get them in a role more suited to their skills and experience, the problem will be solved." When we identify a performance issue as someone being in the wrong role and don't analyze the situation more deeply, we may fall victim to this bias.

Most notably, seeing beyond surface-level people issues can be challenging because it requires leaders to confront the possibility that they are contributing to the problem. Upon deeper examination, we may uncover a tough truth: the individual's performance could have been significantly better if they had been operating within healthier conditions. This introspection demands humility and courage as it requires leaders to acknowledge their roles in shaping the circumstances that led to the issue. The difficulty of leaning into this type of introspection helps explain why so many leaders blame the individual.

## We're Too Busy Fighting Fires

For most leaders, our list of responsibilities is getting longer, our schedules are getting fuller, and we rarely have big chunks of time to dedicate to strategic work. As soon as we solve one urgent problem, two more arise. When this way of working is the norm, finding time to understand and respond to what's at the root of a big issue feels impossible. Looking deeper requires time and mental capacity, and because we anticipate that any worthy solution would require a significant workload as well, we table what we know to be important work. The bottom line: If we don't have that kind of margin, it's easier to blame the surface issue.

To make matters worse, many work cultures reward people's ability to respond effectively to urgent issues, creating an incentive to regularly prioritize whatever is on fire, regardless of importance. When teams spend most of their time firefighting, they don't have the capacity to examine the sources of their fires.

In an environment like this, teams have little space for post-mortems or retrospectives that would offer insights into deeper causes. Without intentional efforts to carve out time for reflection and analysis, the cycle of reactive problem-solving perpetuates itself.

◆ ◆ ◆

Here's the thing: the communication, decision-making, and performance of the people working inside our organizations are and must always be a part of problem diagnosis. That's because, when it comes to what drives organizational success, people are the lifeblood. But when we disproportionately emphasize the role of people in trying to explain the issues we face as leaders, we're ignoring an essential part of the story—and the solution. Even dream teams will burn out and fall short of their performance goals if they find themselves facing an unrelenting set of substandard working conditions. This is why we need a *new lens*.

# The Big Reframe

If we are going to overcome the forces that make it easy to blame people and keep us in a reactionary way of working, we must reframe how we look at issues inside the workplace. In his book *Upstream: The Quest to Solve Problems Before They Happen*, Dan Heath defines "going upstream" as a metaphor for addressing problems at their source rather than reacting to symptoms downstream. As leaders, if we only respond to downstream issues, we miss the opportunity to solve the more significant problems that lie upstream. To disrupt the pattern of misdiagnosing systems problems as people problems, leaders must work against the forces that keep them downstream and begin understanding problems at their roots.

Let's revisit the example of the tech product company CEO who is frustrated with Mark for what she thinks is an inability to prioritize and execute. Initially, she limits her exploration of the issue to a reactive, surface-level analysis of the recent series of events related to Mark's performance. But what if instead of quickly deciding that her issue is Mark, she asked herself and then her executive team, including Mark, two key questions to move their analysis upstream: "Are we aligned on our priorities? How clear and effective have we been at communicating our priorities to each team in the company?" In doing so, the CEO will likely uncover a better explanation for the tension she and Mark are feeling. She might discover:

- The executive team lacks agreed-upon norms and decision protocols for what to do when the more urgent issues of the day compete with their set priorities.
- The CEO recognizes that she continues to struggle with clear communication, leaving the team misaligned on key processes and ownership.
- The priorities of department teams are demanding Mark's attention, but the executive team is entirely unaware of what those priorities are.
- Mark finds the skill of delegation more challenging in a fast-paced environment, and it significantly impacts his ability to be effective.

What the CEO observes as she moves her analysis upstream is the presence of both people issues *and* systems issues. The CEO recognizes her own struggles with communication and also identifies Mark's need to improve his delegation skills. Alongside those individual areas for growth, gaps exist within the team's organizational systems related to process, prioritization, and alignment. Only when leaders go upstream can they see a more accurate picture of what's contributing to the tension, inefficiency, and other performance gaps downstream. And what leaders find when *going upstream* becomes their default practice is a simple yet profound big reframe: **At the heart of work are people *and* systems.**

> # At the heart of work are people and systems.

When leaders begin asking upstream questions in pursuit of discerning what's at the root of their issues, they find this two-dimensional frame: people and systems.

People are at the heart of work because their joy, fulfillment, and engagement are requirements for success—both the individual's and the organization's. It's people who are responsible for defining an organization's Identity and vision. It's people who are responsible for deciding an organization's strategy and designing its systems. And it's people who are responsible for the communication, decision-making, and leadership required of any organization. However, surrounding the actions, ambitions, and behaviors of people inside every organization are systems. Systems are at the heart of work because they impact everything from the norms and expectations guiding the behaviors of employees to the structures and routines that inform how work is executed. It's systems that influence how decisions are made, how goals are set, and who's involved in the process. And it's the continuous influence of systems that ultimately shapes the conditions and culture inside the workplace—whether we as leaders like it or not.

There is an overarching concept that we hope will inspire better systems and more engaged people', and that concept is called an organizational operating system. In this book, we'll further define this foundational, all-encompassing system inherent to every organization that has ever existed, and we'll walk you through a framework, the 6 Levers, designed for leaders who would like to get the most out of their own org OS.

# The Organizational Operating System

To understand what an organizational operating system is and how it works, let's start by looking at how a computer's operating system works.

You might not understand what a computer's operating system does exactly, but you've heard of Microsoft Windows and Mac OS. Designed meticulously by top computer engineers, these underlying systems operate largely in the background, ensuring seamless interactions of a computer's core components. As users, we're used to regular upgrades to the OS and prompt fixes to any glitches, often unaware of the intricate workings behind the scenes.

Before the invention of the computer OS, computing was fragmented and highly inefficient. Each program operated in isolation, lacking cohesion and coordination. Tasks were manual, time-consuming, and prone to error, hindering productivity and innovation.

The invention of the operating system transformed computing. The operating system became the underlying control mechanism for the computer, helping the hardware and software to work together and streamline processes. This new holistic framework led to a better user experience and an era of unprecedented productivity, consistency, and continuous improvement. The OS laid the foundation for the digital world we live in today.

Organizations and teams also have underlying systems, whether or not we're aware of them. This different type of operating system informs everything about how organizations run, from how teams behave and how we make decisions to how we run meetings and how we set goals. An organization's OS is every bit as vital to the performance of an organization as a computer's OS is to its performance.

> **Organizational Operating System (org OS)**: The set of norms, structures, practices, and routines that define how a group of people works together

What does this OS have to do with building healthy teams? Everything. Every team and organization has an organizational operating system—the difference between one organization and another is simply the degree to which each team's org OS has been designed and implemented more intentionally versus more accidentally. Dr. W. Edwards Deming famously said, "Every system is perfectly designed to get the result it gets," which means the overall health of an organization is directly connected to the overall intentionality and effectiveness of the organizational operating system. To build a healthy organization, 'teams must intentionally design, implement, and continuously evolve their organizational OS.

As for computers, during the design process of an operating system, teams start by defining a set of system requirements, a list of features they want the OS to include. When the developers build the OS, they work deliberately to meet these specific system requirements. This collaborative process ensures the computer's OS will be designed to do precisely what the team wants and expects it to do.

The problem with many organizational operating systems is that no one has gone through this type of design process, defining what they want the system to do. As a result, the underlying system that defines how work works is left to develop on its own, without a clear understanding of what the team wants the system to do.

For most teams, the parts of the org OS they interact with the most are running on default. Decision-making protocols, meeting agendas, and even annual goal-setting processes are often more accidental than intentional. Even though most people are highly unsatisfied with the effectiveness of these aspects of their org OS, they rarely prioritize improving them. Most don't realize they have the power to do so.

Similar to a computer's OS, an org OS should be deliberately designed to meet the unique requirements of the organization or team it serves. In our work with hundreds of organizations, we've identified a set of foundational system requirements that are important for most organizations to address as they design a healthy, well-functioning org OS. You might think of this as an initial checklist of items to collaboratively define as you strive toward a more intentionally designed org OS:

- A clearly defined organizational Identity (i.e., mission, beliefs, and values)
- A clear approach to strategic planning
- A routine way to define and set targets for key performance measures
- A methodology for setting and monitoring organizational and team priorities, both long- and short-term
- Clearly established communication norms and tools for efficient collaboration
- Well-designed meeting structures across teams
- A defined operating cycle or annual calendar with meeting protocols for both annual and quarterly review and retrospective meetings
- A common framework for delivering feedback
- Established and shared norms and protocols for conflict resolution
- A systematic approach to leadership development

As teams begin to make progress on the list and move from a more accidental way of working to a more deliberate and intentional way of working, they will quickly witness first-hand the value of a meaningfully defined org OS. The checklist represents a guide to help teams get started in developing their org OS, but it's certainly not an exhaustive list. Teams will realize the most benefit of their org OS when they see it as an evolutionary system with a constant opportunity to further develop and improve it.

While we all know that a computer has an operating system, most people don't recognize the role of the org OS for their team. And it's this lack of awareness that fuels some of our most significant organizational health issues. How can a team build organizational health if they don't actively engage with the underlying system that most significantly contributes to it? Without awareness of their org OS, organizations run on autopilot, regularly confronting inefficiency and conflict and operating in a reactive way of working. Investing in an organizational operating system is not just about improving efficiency—it's about empowering teams with the tools and resources they need to thrive and continuously adapt.

## With and For People

In our experience, no variable has been more influential in the effectiveness of an organizational operating system than people. If we want to build enduring organizational health, we must move the org OS from the background to the foreground and begin designing it with intention. Just as important is how leaders center and involve people in developing their org OS. To unlock the full potential of a more intentional org OS, leaders must embrace a key design principle: *with and for people*. "With people" means thoughtfully and regularly engaging those who will operate within the system in the design process and have an active role in shaping how work works. "For people" means designing ways of working that prioritizes fundamental human needs. When people are involved in defining how work works, they are more engaged and their organizations are more resilient. And when we've designed our operating systems to better meet human needs, we create the conditions in which people can thrive.

We cannot overstate the importance of the *with and for* principle. Leaders could put in an incredible amount of thoughtful effort toward improving their org OS, but if they're not as thoughtful about how they include people in the process, they are far more likely to fail over time. Their teams might comply for a season, but the staying power of the changed systems will quickly fade. Empowering people to be a part of improving the very systems they interact with day in and day out is both investing in people and liberating for the people, and it will cause everyone to want to continuously revisit their org OS. When the systems are designed to meet human needs such as clarity, autonomy, and contribution, no one will need to be told of their value; it will be obvious to everyone.

# The New Base Camp

To realize a team's full potential and finally be able to tackle the root of the issues rather than symptoms, leaders must establish a new base camp upstream and begin intentionally designing their org OS. Your journey begins here.

In the following chapters, we'll lay out a framework for your org OS—the 6 Levers—and walk through each major component of the system a step at a time, helping you understand why it's important and how you can get started.

# The 6 Levers Framework

Raise your hand if any of these scenarios sound familiar, whether in your present or past workplace:

- Communication norms are inconsistent, leading to an ineffective flow of key information and feelings of frustration.
- Meetings feel like default gatherings with no clear agendas, resulting in directionless discussions without clear outcomes.
- Immediate needs or the influence of vocal individuals drive decision-making processes rather than taking a more inclusive approach.
- Roles, responsibilities, and organizational charts lack clear rationale, having evolved reactively through seasons, leading to significant cynicism in their value.
- The mission and core values don't resonate and are largely dormant, making it difficult for people to find meaning in their work.
- Resistance to change stifles innovation and adaptation.
- Teams prioritize established norms and routines over new, potentially more effective practices, hindering growth and agility.

If any of these scenarios sound familiar, you are most likely experiencing a gap in your team's organizational operating system. To be clear, every organization has parts of its org OS that run more accidentally. It's not a matter of having an accidental or intentional org OS; instead, it's about identifying those areas that have been running on default for a while and prioritizing where you need to bring increased intention.

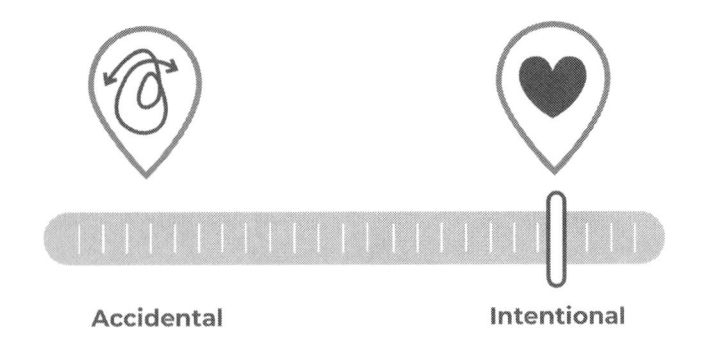

**Accidental**          **Intentional**

THE 6 LEVERS FRAMEWORK

# A More Intentional Org OS

Intentionality means developing new ways of working with clear objectives in mind. As we mentioned in Chapter 1, it begins with first recognizing that you have an org OS. Once you have embraced this important first step, you can then decide which aspects of it you want to begin improving. If your weekly team meetings feel unproductive, step back and align with your purpose, then begin redesigning your meetings to achieve that purpose. Odds are, many of the work systems you interact with the most have been running on default for a while. Through intentional efforts over time, you will find yourself working in an org OS that looks like the list described in the "Signs of an Intentionally Designed Org OS" box.

> **Signs of an Intentionally Designed Org OS**
>
> - Team members understand and are energized by the organization's Identity. They pass every decision, small or large, through this filter.
> - Teams seek to go upstream to proactively address issues at their root cause.
> - Teams leverage more than just meetings to collaborate, designing strong synchronous and asynchronous ways of working that are energizing instead of draining.
> - Leaders are self-aware and vulnerable, and they have the tools and skills to effectively coach employees. Everyone has access to development opportunities.
> - Teams embrace a growth mindset and a spirit of experimentation.
> - Teams have tools and practices to navigate conflict or tension, and as a result, they are able to build trust and resiliency.

Now, doesn't that list sound like an organization everyone would want to work for? In organizations that have intentionally developed an org OS, a leader no longer worries about being involved in every major decision or driving focus across multiple teams. They have confidence in their 'teams' abilities to set priorities, run great meetings, and work through conflicts. Intentional leaders can be more present with each person and in each moment because they have space to be proactive instead of reactive. Leaders have the peace that comes from knowing their teams are operating on an ever-strengthening system. They no longer feel a rush of anxiety when someone knocks on their door.

# The Power of a Framework

We talked in Chapter 1 about how system-level problems require system-level solutions. Within an organization, leaders cannot expect to address systemic or structural issues with one-off fixes. They need a more intentional organizational operating system. However, this idea is conceptual and remains a bit elusive without more concrete structure and language. This is why we built a framework.

Before we get into the 6 Levers framework, let's touch on why the Levers are part of a framework and why you need a framework (we all do) to guide the process of building organizational health.

A framework is powerful for several reasons, including those shown in this graphic.

### The Power of a Framework

| | |
|---|---|
| **Clarity** | A framework provides a structured approach to navigating complex issues, creating a shared mental model that streamlines communication and decision-making. When a team uses a shared framework, they're able to work from a clear set of criteria and standards that everyone is aware of. |
| **Common Language** | In today's organizations, it can feel like everyone is speaking a different language. A shared framework serves as a common language to address issues, evaluate opportunities, and determine strategy. When everyone has shared language to describe abstract concepts, it's easier to get the team on the same page. |
| **Autonomy** | Good frameworks empower teams with a sense of autonomy, allowing them to navigate challenges effectively while aligning with the organization's mission and strategic goals. In essence, good frameworks don't just guide. They liberate teams, fostering a sense of ownership and self-directed problem-solving. |
| **Actionable** | A framework transforms abstract concepts into actionable steps, enabling organizations to achieve enduring health, close execution gaps, and drive meaningful progress. Each actionable step has the potential to build momentum, leading to meaningful progress. |

An intentionally designed organizational operating system has incredible power to build organizational health and close the execution gap. But the next question becomes, "How do we do that?" Teams need an approachable, easy-to-understand framework to help them intentionally design their operating system. This is why we created the 6 Levers, a framework to equip teams with simple, actionable tools and practices that allow them to go upstream and build better ways of working.

# Welcome to the 6 Levers

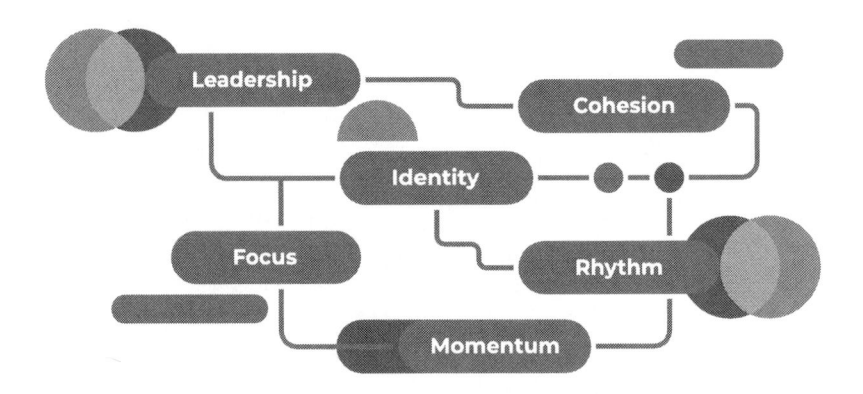

*Diagram showing the 6 Levers: Leadership, Cohesion, Identity, Focus, Rhythm, Momentum*

If you talk with a thousand leaders—from major global nonprofits to purpose-centered start-ups—about their biggest challenges, a lot of what you'll hear will center around one major theme. They are struggling with a reactionary way of working. They feel like they don't own their time and that they have to choose between having a healthy culture and getting the results they want.

These struggles have a pattern. We see them repeatedly, yet they are largely preventable. Understanding these patterns and struggles led us to create a framework that addresses each of these blockers one by one. What emerged is the 6 Levers. Each Lever is both an indicator of team health and a Lever leaders can pull to build health.

We'll walk through an overview of all six in this chapter so you can understand them enough to know which Levers your organization needs to address the most. In the next six chapters, we'll cover the Levers one by one and show you how to begin moving upstream, bringing greater intention to how you design your organizational operating system.

# Identity

**The Identity Lever:** A set of core beliefs, values, and principles that define an organization's essence, purpose, and *identity*, serving as the foundation upon which the organization operates and evolves.

Identity captures the soul of the team or organization: what it believes, why it exists, and what it values. It clarifies an organization's "why" and aligns stakeholders with the organization's deepest purpose and convictions. An organization's Identity serves as the foundation upon which the rest of the organization is built. When Identity is strong, it becomes a compass, guiding the vision and acting as a filter for strategic decisions. Identity clarifies the type of organization you want to be and provides a way for teams to build purposeful ways of working that honor their most important values and operating tenets.

## Why it's worth investing in:

- It helps teams find a real sense of meaning in their work.
- It informs team habits, giving them a much higher chance of sticking because of their depth of meaning.
- It unlocks purposeful and intentional growth.
- It offers a framework for decision-making that is clear, transparent, and tethered to a deep sense of purpose.
- It attracts people who are aligned and repels people who aren't.

### Indicators that Identity needs investment:

- The mission, values, and beliefs are only understood by a few. Team members are largely unable to recite or recall them.
- A gap exists between the defined identity and the reality of what it feels like working in the culture.
- Vision doesn't feel purposeful or inspiring because it's not aligned with a deeper "why."
- Employees are not values-aligned.
- Employees lean on their personal values and beliefs, which leads to recurring, unresolved tension.

# Leadership

**The Leadership Lever:** A set of tools, practices, and mindsets that empower individuals at all levels to lead with purpose, confidence, and effectiveness, fostering a culture of empowerment, growth, and *leadership*.

The Leadership Lever is grounded in an unwavering belief in human potential. It's about recognizing that leadership isn't a position—it's a quality inherent in everyone. It's about fostering an environment where each person, regardless of their title or role, feels empowered to lead in their unique way. The Leadership Lever involves embracing essential practices such as curiosity, self-awareness, and vulnerability. It also involves creating psychologically safe environments that lead to deeper engagement and adaptability. When Leadership is strong, teams will recognize and tap into the potential of every individual, creating a culture of collaboration, innovation, and continuous improvement.

## Why it's worth investing in:

- It ensures that leadership is developed as a quality within everyone, not just people in management roles.
- It helps leaders work to understand and address the unique human needs of team members.
- It teaches leaders to see themselves as coaches to their team members.
- It creates a culture of experimentation and feedback that results in the ability to continuously learn and adapt.
- It helps leaders become more self-aware, open-minded, and growth-oriented.

## Indicators that Leadership needs investment:

- Organizations view leadership as an expectation of only managers, not all employees.
- Organizations limit development opportunities to managers only.
- Organizations lack appreciation for the outsized influence that managers have on employee engagement and the role of employee engagement on overall organizational health.
- Team leaders and managers aren't committed to developing themselves and exhibit low self-awareness and curiosity.
- Leaders direct and give advice instead of listening, teaching, and coaching.

## Focus

**The Focus Lever:** The tools, practices, and mindsets that enable teams to navigate complexity, prioritize effectively, and *focus* their efforts on strategic objectives, ensuring alignment, clarity, and impact.

The Focus Lever equips teams to navigate the complex nature of collaborative work and elevate priorities, targets, and strategies that matter most. By accessing the Focus Lever, teams can identify what matters most and channel their best resources there. The result is a feeling of freedom as teams are encouraged and empowered to invest their time and energy in the work that matters most to them. The Focus Lever consists of establishing priorities and vitals targets at the organizational and team levels with both near-term and long-term time horizons. When Focus is strong, teams experience heightened innovation and collaboration on their most important work, and they feel energized by it because they know the significant impact it's making.

### Why it's worth investing in:

- It equips people to focus on the most important work.
- It increases engagement because people can see how their efforts are contributing to the most important work.
- It highlights where to focus at different time horizons, both in the near term and annually.
- It enables collaboration and innovation because teams are empowered to take ownership of their priorities.

### Indicators that Focus needs investment:

- Teams lack clarity on priorities or have too many priorities for their capacity.
- Team members have out-of-control to-do lists with mostly urgent but not important work.
- Teams have a habit of abandoning older priorities to chase new, seemingly exciting ideas.
- Priorities are quickly abandoned.
- Teams do not pair priorities with intentionally designed Rhythms to monitor, adjust, and learn from.

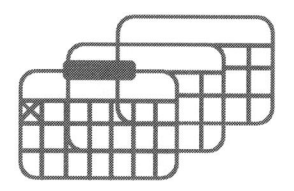

# Rhythm

**The Rhythm Lever:** The intentional set of routines and planning cycles that establish a meaningful and disciplined operational *rhythm* within teams and across the entire organization, fostering alignment, accountability, and focus.

The Rhythm Lever leverages the power of habit to ensure the most essential strategic activities are not left subject to chance. By thoughtfully designing their habits, teams can move out of the default, accidental way of operating and into an intentional way of working, engineered to achieve their goals. The more automatic teams can make these routine activities, the less effort it will take to sustain them. The Rhythm Lever includes meetings designed to achieve specific objectives, recurring communications aimed at driving clarity and collaboration, and repeatable processes that need thoughtful design and documentation. When Rhythm is strong, teams feel like they are focusing on their most important, high-impact work because they have intentionally designed ways of working that prioritize them, ensuring they can rise above a state of day-to-day firefighting.

## Why it's worth investing in:

- It ensures the team has dedicated time on a regular basis to collaboratively resolve emergent issues.
- It creates a system for each team to regularly review and reference priorities.
- It helps avoid unnecessary meetings.
- It creates dynamic and engaging meetings that team members enjoy.
- It enables teams to integrate strategic work into the day-to-day.

## Indicators that Rhythm needs investment:

- Teams lack consistent habits.
- Teams do not meet regularly, and the meetings they have are not productive, purposeful, and actionable.
- Essential strategic activities (goal-setting, monitoring, prioritizing, and problem-solving) are ineffective, inconsistent, and left to chance.
- Teams rarely leverage asynchronous tools to collaborate.

# Cohesion

**The Cohesion Lever:** A set of structures, tools, and rituals designed to deliberately cultivate strong interpersonal connections, shared experiences, and cohesion within teams.

The Cohesion Lever offers ways for teams to deepen a collective sense of purpose, resolve tension more effectively, and participate in shared experiences that bring them closer together. A couple of the tools and practices in the Cohesion Lever focus on forming team Agreements and developing team Rituals. The Cohesion Lever also appreciates the importance of fostering team psychological safety as a prerequisite to deepening engagement and connectedness. When Cohesion is high, teams have the ability to navigate change and drive progress because they trust each other and have a deep, shared conviction in the impact they are making together.

## Why it's worth investing in:

- It enables a thriving culture that makes progress possible.
- It creates the conditions for team members to thrive and feel joy at work.
- It helps build team trust and psychological safety.
- It creates a sense of belonging and shared purpose in a team.
- It offers a way for teams to resolve recurring tension and conflict.

### Indicators that Cohesion needs investment:

- Team members have anything less than high trust.
- Leaders struggle to see the connection between trusting, cohesive teams and meeting fundamental human needs.
- The team has low psychological safety. People rarely take chances or share candidly.
- The team has little to no feeling of a shared purpose or sense of belonging.
- The team struggles to effectively address conflict or resolve tensions.

## Momentum

**The Momentum Lever:** A set of tools, structures, and mindsets designed to accelerate progress, foster continuous learning, and cultivate a culture of feedback and experimentation that leads to a strong sense of organizational *momentum.*

When teams access the Momentum Lever, they can cultivate a culture of experimentation and iterative progress that works to overcome the fear of trying new ideas. It can be an incredible catalyst for progress and innovation. They learn to celebrate successes and failures, seeing the value of learning in both. To avoid analysis paralysis, they promote a culture of action with mantras like "good enough for now, safe enough to try." The tools and practices within the Momentum Lever include creating a culture of feedback, running team retrospectives, limiting work in progress, and learning to embrace small wins. When Momentum is strong, teams see and feel consistent and regular progress, which acts as fuel to inspire them to reach new heights.

## Why it's worth investing in:

- It teaches teams how to implement changes that will stick.
- It creates a culture where feedback is normal.
- It equips the team to navigate rapid change in a dynamic world.
- It encourages a culture of learning where it feels safe to make mistakes.
- It enables the organization to constantly evolve as it learns and implements new practices.

## Indicators that Momentum needs investment:

- Leaders value rigorous analysis more than progress and action.
- Feedback is rare, and when it happens, people are ill-equipped to give and receive it.
- Continuous learning is referenced, but there are no' systems that allow it to take place.
- The culture doesn't allow for experimentation and learning through doing.
- A "commitment to excellence" is a cover-up for perfectionist tendencies that lead to organizational inertia.

◆ ◆ ◆

## It's Your Org OS

The 6 Levers framework provides the organizational infrastructure for any team seeking to design their org OS with more intention. The framework also offers insight into the overall health of your team, with each Lever representing a key dimension of organizational health. The common language this establishes for teams cannot be underestimated. Not only does adopting the framework enable more focused and collaborative discussion on how to further develop your org OS, but it also creates an evergreen lens for evaluating the health of your team. With a shared understanding of each Lever, teams begin to notice when "'focus is low'" or when their "'rhythm feels off'," and they immediately return to their OS to discern how they might improve.

Earlier, we talked about awareness and how a lack of awareness and understanding surrounding the role of your org OS is often the root of your team's recurring and most damaging issues. By adopting the framework, awareness skyrockets, enabling teams to disrupt these patterns and immediately realize the benefits of this new system touching all aspects of their work. In the chapters that follow, we'll offer more insight into each Lever and why it's such an important part of your team's health. We'll also share a handful of actionable tools and practices that you can use to build more intentionality and health into your org OS and within your team. But here's the thing: You can strengthen your team's health in each area in countless ways, and our intention with this book is not to provide a comprehensive playbook or even suggest "'best practices'." Instead, our hope is that teams will feel inspired to become stewards of a more intentional organizational operating system and consider the 6 Levers as a foundation for developing it.

To help stamp this core idea, consider your own health and well-being. You might break it down into four core areas: physical, mental, spiritual, and emotional health. As you consider how you might improve your personal health in any one of these areas, it's likely that your approach would look different than someone else's and yet be equally effective. You can think about improving the intentionality of your org OS and the health of your team in a similar way. This is why we encourage teams to think of the framework as a strategic guide and the foundation of their org OS, *even over* an actionable set of tools and practices to serve as a proven playbook. Do we offer a set of tools and practices to serve your implementation? Of course! And we share these strategies humbly, knowing they are not the superior and singular way to build organizational health.

Unlike many frameworks, there is not one way to adopt the 6 Levers framework, nor is there a single, proven path to developing your org OS with intention. What's most important is for teams to find an approach that works for them. It's *your* org OS. As you begin to define your organizational operating system, we offer you a handful of guiding principles:

- **It's evolutionary.** The way you define the various components of your org OS should continuously evolve as your team learns and grows. The first few times that you bring more intention to your org OS, you may not see immediate progress. In fact, you might sense resistance and tension, as with most change efforts. To overcome this friction, teams must embrace an evolutionary mindset, understanding that through experimentation and incremental adjustments toward more intentionality, your system will grow stronger and more meaningfully defined over time. Rarely does a single tool or process transform the way your team works; however, a mindset and commitment to keep making it better will bring successful results. Over time, your ways of working will indeed transform dramatically, but it's much more likely that a series of small steps will get you there in a way that one big leap could not achieve.
- **It's collaboratively developed.** 6 Levers was designed to engage the entire team, not just the leaders. All too often, change efforts

and strategies are only carried by the top levels of leadership, with only minimal inclusion of the rest of the organization. This is a mistake, as team members at all levels of the organization are vital to executing strategy and building a healthy culture. As you work to implement 6 Levers in your organization, it may start with the leadership team, but it must continue from there. The practices and tools you find are applicable to all levels of teams throughout an organization.

- **It's your org OS.** Instead of implementing a strict guidebook, the goal is for teams to develop and take ownership of *their unique* org OS. If you were to observe any three organizations running on 6 Levers, they might appear similar from thirty thousand feet. But zoom in, and you will see clear differences based on decisions they've made for *their teams*. It's not a paint-by-number model. Building a strong and resilient org OS stems from appreciating the unique strengths, challenges, and preferences of your team and designing your system in response. Most importantly, it demands that teams design their org OS inclusively.

Keep this guidance in mind as you begin developing your org OS with the 6 Levers framework. Now that you have been introduced to each of the 6 Levers and understand what an org OS is and why it's important to design yours with intention, let's take a deeper look at each Lever, beginning with Identity.

# Identity

# Identity

A 2018 *Harvard Business Review* article reported that—out of two thousand people surveyed—nine out of ten were willing to trade a percentage of their lifetime earnings for greater meaning at work. How much would they trade? A shockingly high 23%. The writers jokingly concluded that the twenty-first-century list of essentials should be updated to "food, clothing, shelter—and meaningful work."

For a leader trying to build a healthy culture while also driving results, creating "meaningful work" can feel incredibly challenging. How does one go about making work meaningful? To begin to answer this question, we turn to the Identity Lever.

One of the most impactful ways to strengthen employee engagement is to enable people to discover more purpose and meaning in their work. Strong organizational Identity clarifies why the organization exists and what it believes, creating a bridge for any employee to connect with that purpose. A clear and meaningful Identity also fosters a sense of belonging on a team, allowing employees to clearly grasp what they are a part of and encouraging camaraderie because the team feels they are an important part of a mission that's meaningful and larger than themselves. A shared sense of purpose at the Identity level has the power to translate into a shared sense of purpose at the day-to-day work level. As one's sense of purpose and contribution grows, so, too, does their commitment and drive, leading to increased employee engagement.

When Identity is strong, organizations can cultivate a work environment that is not only more meaningful and fulfilling for individuals but also establishes a cohesive force propelling the team toward shared goals.

Also, Identity gives workers a navigational guide that lines up their personal values and beliefs with the organization's mission and values. When the employee and the organization's Identity are aligned, it helps the person feel a profound sense of purpose. It also brings team members together so they are cohesive in their work. Plus, it's motivating. Everyone feels more resilient and adaptable when their Identity guides their actions and decisions.

## More Than a Mission

Warby Parker, the online eyeglasses retailer, is a great example of a company that has thoughtfully taken the time to clarify their organizational Identity. Most "about us" sections of company websites aren't clear. They tend to feature corporate jargon or vague positive statements that don't mean much. Warby Parker's, however, shows the intentionality the company has brought to defining what it believes, why it exists, and the type of organization it seeks to be. It reads:

> *Warby Parker was founded with a mission: to inspire and impact the world with vision, purpose, and style. We're constantly asking ourselves how we can do more and make a greater impact—and that starts by reimagining everything that a company and industry can be. We want to demonstrate that a business can scale, be profitable, and do good in the world—without charging a premium for it. And we've learned that it takes creativity, empathy, and innovation to achieve that goal.*

They've clarified their initial convictions that inspired the founding of the company. They've developed values that are written in unique, plain language that everyone can relate to. They've elevated the importance of their "buy one, give one" model throughout their business operations. The site shows the founders' favorite books, their sense of humor, and what it feels like to work there. Clarifying its Identity offered a strong foundation for incredible growth as Warby Parker grew to 1,400 employees in its first eight years.

But they didn't stop at clarifying their Identity. They brought to life this clarity and conviction to create a more Identity-centered culture. Here are a few ways they intentionally activate their Identity:

- *Values:* Related to their value of "Learn, Engage, Repeat," they have an open library where employees are encouraged to drop in and read.
- *Elevating connection:* Driven by an operational belief that building strong, personal connections fosters a more cohesive and engaged community, they developed an immersive employee onboarding experience that involves people throughout the organization, beyond HR.
- *Measuring engagement:* Every week, employees fill out a simple Happiness Pulse Survey to help leaders proactively respond to negative trends.
- *Intentional meeting design:* Leaders source weekly innovation ideas from anyone who wants to submit them. Most remarkably, the company still runs the same weekly all-hands meeting it has from the beginning. Leaders strongly feel that it helps them stay connected and responsive to competitive pressures.

When it comes to building strong, resilient teams, there's no better place to start than intentionally helping people find meaning in their work. While bringing clarity and meaning to your organizational Identity is not the only requirement to help people find meaning in their work, it is the foundation. When it comes to clarifying Identity, nearly every organization acknowledges its importance, yet few orgs see it as an imperative for advancing their vision and building enduring organizational health.

In the article, "How to Connect Your Employees to Purpose," Hubert Joly shares that when CEOs were asked to rate the importance of having and living a great corporate purpose to the success of their company, their average response was 9.1 out of 10. However when they were asked how alive the purpose is in their company, they only rated it 6 out of 10. It's clear that having a well-defined and alive organizational purpose is foundational to meaningful work.

**A robust Identity is not just an internal compass; it's a broadcast signal.** It echoes beyond the walls of the organization, creating a unique frequency where both insiders and outsiders are tuned in and engaging with the organization with a deeper, more meaningful connection.

## When Identity Is Strong

When a team's Identity is clear and meaningful, progress is unlocked in a powerful way.

Beyond connecting each employee to a sense of meaning, a clear Identity increases the likelihood that teams will adopt purposeful habits. It becomes the guiding force behind the growth paths chosen by organizations, equipping teams with greater determination as they pursue them. A well-defined Identity provides a set of strategic decision-making criteria, acting as a reliable compass in the dynamic and ever-changing world. Clarity of Identity emerges as a catalyst for organizational cohesion, habit formation, strategic resilience, and effective decision-making.

### Strong Identity

- Enables purposeful org OS design
- Unlocks intentional growth
- Acts as strategic decision-making criteria

# Enabling Purposeful Org OS Design

In his book *Atomic Habits: An Easy & Proven Way to Build Good Habits & Break Bad Ones*, James Clear underscores the critical role of Identity in the establishment of lasting habits. According to Clear, the first step in making habits stick is to clearly define our Identity. For instance, individuals who perceive themselves as healthy are more likely to adopt and sustain healthy habits. Conversely, if a person decides to incorporate a new habit, such as attending a yoga class three times a week, without a deep connection to an existing belief, the habit is less likely to endure.

This principle extends beyond personal habits to organizational behavior. When teams adopt new habits that lack a connection to their collective Identity, they are on unstable ground. In the face of increased demands, there may be a temptation to discard a habit. However, if the habit is explicitly linked to a core tenet, it is more likely to endure. It's important to note that sticking with a habit doesn't preclude adjustments. Teams may need to refine their habits to better serve their evolving needs, but outright abandonment becomes less likely.

Consider the following example that illustrates this concept, based on one of our 'team's tenets and associated habits:

**Tenet: We collaboratively shape the way work works.**

**Habit: We set short-term priorities and agreements as a team every two months.**

Now, envision a busy season, prompting a search for time-saving measures. A team member suggests reconsidering the full team involvement in the bi-monthly planning day. Another team member, recalling the team's tenet about shaping collaborative work, interjects,

"But, that seems inconsistent with our tenet." The initial proposer, realizing the misalignment, might respond, "You're right. That's not the right area to get time back. Let's explore other options."

It's essential to recognize that tenets aren't the sole source for teams to ground their habits. They can also draw on their beliefs, values, and vitals as a robust foundation. Teams often face an Identity crises when adopting practices that lack a clear source of inspiration. Over time, the rationale for these practices becomes murky, resulting in a fractured culture. Purposefully connecting ways of working to Identity fosters an intentional and cohesive culture, driving high engagement and a strong sense of ownership among team members.

## Unlocking Intentional Growth

Several years ago, our team was guiding a client through the development of a new strategic vision. As part of our discovery, we asked them to share any previous strategic plans and any artifacts that would help us understand their Identity. They told us that we could find their mission statement on their website, and that was the extent of their documented Identity.

As we began to interview and hold focus groups with people throughout the organization, we heard many different versions of the organization's Identity. We also heard people use their individual beliefs to fill the gaps where the organization was unclear. As we listened to what they thought the organization's Identity was, the team varied widely in their Theory of Impact, values, tenets, and vitals. As a result, when we asked them about their vision for where they wanted to be in three years, the responses were all over the place. It was clear to us that they needed to clarify their Identity before they could cast their vision for the next three years.

When teams launch into casting vision without first understanding their Identity, they put many areas at risk:

- *Misalignment of Goals:* Without a clear understanding of the organization's Identity, its vision may not align with its core values, beliefs, and purpose. This misalignment can lead to confusion and conflict among team members, hindering progress.
- *Lack of Employee Engagement:* Employees are more likely to be engaged and motivated when they can see a clear connection between the organizational vision and their own values. Without understanding the Identity, the vision may not resonate with the workforce, leading to reduced enthusiasm and commitment.
- *Resistance to Change:* If the vision requires significant changes in behavior, processes, or strategies, employees may resist the changes if they perceive them as incompatible with the organization's Identity, which is much more likely if it hasn't been clarified. Resistance can impede progress toward the envisioned future.

Teams that have a clear and documented Identity are much more likely to make progress toward their vision for several reasons, including:

1. **Alignment of Purpose:** Understanding organizational Identity helps align the vision with the core purpose, values, and beliefs of the organization. When the vision resonates with the Identity, employees are more likely to connect with it on a personal level and feel purpose and commitment.
2. **Easier Implementation of Change:** Vision often involves change and adaptation. When the vision is rooted in the organization's Identity, employees are more likely to embrace and support the necessary changes, seeing them as an organic evolution rather than a disruptive force.
3. **Increased Resilience:** Organizations that have a strong sense of Identity are often more resilient in the face of challenges. When the vision is integrated with the organizational Identity, it becomes a guiding force that helps the organization navigate uncertainties,

adapt to changes, and persevere in pursuit of its goals.

## Strategic Decision-Making Criteria

**When Identity is clear and communicated well, it acts as a guide for decision-making, both in evaluating new ideas and initiatives and in day-to-day operations.**

When Identity is clear and felt, teams can regularly reference it as they make decisions, both big and small. They will naturally look for harmony between their decisions and their Identity. When this happens, it leads to a strong sense of alignment within and across teams.

Decision-making also becomes more efficient. The clarity provided by the organizational Identity streamlines the decision-making process, reducing ambiguity and facilitating quicker and more decisive actions.

Employees and external stakeholders often gain confidence in organizations with a strong Identity-driven decision-making approach. Consistent decisions reflective of the organizational Identity build trust and credibility. They communicate that an organization is walking its talk.

# The Dimensions of Identity

Now we're getting to the "how" part of creating a strong and healthy Identity in an org OS. It's more than a mission statement. Organizations can create a more holistic picture of Identity by developing six dimensions. These dimensions are captured within a tool called the Compass (more about the Compass at the end of this chapter).

### The 6 Dimensions of Identity

**Beliefs:** The collection of shared convictions about why an organization exists.

**Mission:** The core purpose that drives an organization.

**Theory of Impact:** The most significant differentiator in how an organization accomplishes its mission.

**Values:** The deeply ingrained behaviors core to an organization's culture that guide all team interactions.

**Vitals:** The core indicators of organizational health and performance, measured in perpetuity.

**Tenets:** The most important principles that guide organizational culture and operations.

This full picture of an org's Identity creates a strong foundation to develop culture and shape operations. Additionally, it will help to guide strategic direction and desired team behavior. We'll share an example of each component in practice and define what it is and why it matters.

# Beliefs: Why Do We Exist?

Sherry works in the backpack department of a large outdoor retailer. The job can be tiring and repetitive, but when Sherry is feeling frustrated at answering the same questions again and again, she calls to mind the company's belief: "We believe that the outdoors should be accessible to everyone." Customers are asking basic questions about which backpack to use because they've never hiked before. By patiently and enthusiastically answering questions and demonstrating features, Sherry is fulfilling the company's belief by helping make the outdoors accessible to new hikers. She knows that if she can make hiking feel less intimidating, it lowers one possible barrier to helping these people experience the outdoors.

## What Are Beliefs?
Beliefs are the three to six essential reasons why the organization exists. They finish the sentence, "We exist because we believe_____."

## Why Beliefs Matter
Typically, organizations are grounded in a set of convictions that sparked their original founding. The challenge lies in the fact that these convictions often aren't clearly documented. Articulating a concise set of beliefs empowers teams to reinforce their purpose with a level of clarity that surpasses the typical mission statement. While a mission statement outlines what an organization exists to achieve, beliefs provide insight into why this objective is meaningful to the organization in the first place, declaring, "We exist because we believe_____."

In the absence of well-defined organizational beliefs, orgs find less alignment and clarity around the core pillars of their existence and leave the routine connection back to this subject to chance. It also leaves their mission statements subject to interpretation. Two organizations could have the exact same mission but serve vastly different purposes. Ideally, the beliefs of each organization would highlight and clarify these differences. Without shared beliefs, individuals have ample room to construct their own narratives around the mission statement, potentially leading to a fragmented organizational culture. This can result in Identity drift over time, ultimately contributing to a less-engaged and less-impactful team.

During challenging periods, leaders must rally around these deeply ingrained beliefs to keep the core purpose at the forefront of their decision-making processes.

**Examples:**

**K–12 School**
- All students can thrive in the right learning environment
- Students learn differently.

**Consulting Group (the 6 Levers team)**
- Human needs should be at the center of organizational design.
- Everyone deserves to find meaning and purpose in their work.

**Locally Sourced Food Delivery Company**
- Accessing local food should be convenient.
- Locally sourced food doesn't have to be expensive.

# Mission: What Is Our Core Purpose?

"How do you think your role connects to our mission?"

Oluwatobi, the director of HR, asks this question of every new employee during their orientation at the ad agency where he works. Usually, the new employees are confused, saying something like, "I'm a receptionist. All I do is answer phones," or "I'm a graphic designer. What does that have to do with the mission?"

"Well, our hope is that every member of our team can see how their role advances our mission," he tells them. "Our mission is to provide purposeful advertising and branding to help our clients grow to new heights. Every employee has a critical role to play in making this happen. We cannot achieve our ultimate goal without a high-performing team working together. So, take a few minutes and consider the question again: "How does your role connect to our mission?"

After a few moments of thought, the new employee offers a tentative answer along the lines of:

"Well, I guess for our clients to be able to connect their products to the people who need them, someone has to connect them with us. So I answer the phone, and it's my job to connect the client to our team."

"Bingo! That's how you connect to our mission," says Oluwatobi.

Employees carry this idea with them throughout their time at the agency, even mentioning in their exit interviews that they were happy to contribute to a mission bigger than themselves.

## What Is a Mission?

A mission is the ultimate objective an organization seeks to achieve. It finishes the sentence, "We exist to achieve the objective to _____."

## Why Mission Matters

A clear, concise, and compelling mission is a powerful tool to align stakeholders with the organization's highest purpose. It also guides focused growth and operates as a point of true north to help teams thoughtfully navigate toward it.

Most organizations have mission statements, but the words don't always resonate with people in a way that builds buy-in and excitement. When a mission isn't regularly referenced, it's because it often has too much jargon. A mission statement should be bold and aspirational yet practical, defining the core purpose that drives the organization.

> **Examples:**
>
> - **Tech Start-Up Incubator:** We exist to build San Antonio one start-up at a time.
> - **Homeless Planning Org:** We exist to make homelessness rare, brief, and non-recurring.
> - **Children's Museum:** We exist to create lifelong memories through joyful learning experiences.

# Theory of Impact: What Is Our Secret Sauce?

Every time Tanisha leads annual planning for her product team at an organic spice company, she starts with a reminder of their Theory of Impact: "We achieve our mission through sustainable, fair partnerships and a fierce commitment to climate justice." She thinks of the Theory of Impact as "rigorous strategic filtering." Every new product feature or launch has to go through the filter of the Theory of Impact. The team knows to expect two questions in response to every new idea: "Is this fair to the farmers?" and "Can we accomplish this without harming the planet?" If the answer is ever "no," the idea goes back to the drawing board.

## What is Theory of Impact?

Theory of Impact defines the overarching "how" and strategy for achieving the mission. It finishes the sentence, "We achieve our mission by _____."

## Why Theory of Impact Matters

Even with a well-articulated mission statement written in plain language that resonates with people, teams can find themselves chasing big strategic objectives that lack a common thread to connect to. A Theory of Impact statement helps organizations clarify specifically how they will achieve their mission. It defines their unique path to success.

Think of your Theory of Impact as the beginning of your strategy. It's the first step to clarify your strategic direction to pursue the mission. Just like the previous example, it can help teams make strategic decisions. Whether considering a new product feature, a new partnership, or a change to an existing product or service, teams should consider, "Does this honor our Theory of Impact?"

### Examples:

- **Leadership Development Group:** Building capacity in leaders by providing easy access to a wide variety of media that features thought leadership from all industries.
- **Veterinary Care Collective of Clinics:** We achieve our mission by embracing the latest technology and focusing our care not just on the animals we treat but also on the human families they live with.
- **Nonprofit Supporting Recovery:** Helping teens and young adults sustain their recovery through engaging in a community of peer support.

# Values: How Do We Behave?

Calvin was both shocked and overjoyed the day his daughter, Rosie, called him out about his screen time. As the CIO of an app company focused on helping people meditate, Calvin was part of the team that chose "Fully present here, fully present at home" as a value. Rosie heard her father reference this value many times without Calvin even realizing she was listening. One evening, Calvin was playing with Rosie on the living room floor and got distracted by the ding of a text. He started texting back, but his wise four-year-old stopped him.

"Daddy," she said, her hand on her hip, "you are not being fully present."

Calvin's wife popped her head in from the kitchen, a wide grin on her face.

"If you're going to talk about these values all the time, you better be living by them, or Chief Values Officer Rosie will get you back in line!"

This is a wonderful example of what's at the heart of work. Yes, it's people and systems, and for Calvin, it's also about being present for his work teams and for his loved ones at home.

## What Are Values
Values are the three to six deeply ingrained behaviors at the heart of an organization's culture that guide all team interactions. They finish the sentence, "The behaviors we value most are _____."

## Why Values Matter
Values that resonate are much more than words on a wall or a webpage. In *The Advantage: Why Organizational Health Trumps Everything Else in Business,* Patrick Lencioni discusses how values are not just a collection of nice sentiments but the embodiment of essential behaviors within organizations. They function as the silent architects shaping the fabric

of an organization's culture, providing a guiding light for actions and acting as a linchpin for overall success and sustainability. Along with tenets, values help an organization define who it wants to be from a behavioral and everyday culture perspective.

When values are well-articulated, they transform into a framework that empowers teams to offer and receive meaningful feedback and coaching. This framework becomes a shared language, allowing team members to assess their behaviors and performance against a set of agreed-upon principles, fostering a culture of continuous improvement.

When values are undefined or ambiguous, feedback and coaching can devolve into subjective assessments based on personal preferences. Without a common set of values to reference, individuals may find themselves critiquing others, not against a collective standard but against individual idiosyncrasies. This lack of clarity makes it challenging to address conflicts, as different team members bring varied expectations regarding the behaviors they anticipate from their colleagues.

### Examples:

- **Relentless Mental Discipline:** We solve problems with creativity, dedication, and diligence.
- **Intentional Presence:** We stay in the present moment because we believe our best work comes when our attention isn't divided.
- **We Before Me:** We put the community first and draw strength from our differences in order to build a stronger ecosystem.

# Vitals: How do we measure organizational health and performance?

Paulo runs an online community for fundraisers. As a small start-up, the team is frequently pulled in many directions. Sometimes, it feels like they're pivoting so fast that they're spinning in circles. It can be hard to judge what's working and what's not, and the team is constantly asking, "Do we need to change course?" In the midst of this chaotic, fast-paced environment, Paulo keeps one vital top of mind at all times: community engagement. It's the sales team's job to bring more users onto the platform. It's his job to keep them happy once they're there. Paulo knows that when his team is doing well, the engagement metric will show how much time each user spends in the community per week. He monitors more granular data, as well, but this is the topline metric that gives him the clearest picture of whether he's succeeding or not.

### What Are Vitals
Vitals are the most essential indicators of team health and performance, measured annually in perpetuity. They finish the sentence, "The metrics that best define our success are _____."

### Why Vitals Matter
When it comes to data, the most successful teams focus on the handful of measures that matter most. Teams must sift through the noise and identify the measures most vital to their team's health and performance. Defining this set of essential indicators creates near-term focus and drives long-term clarity. Vitals are the metrics that always matter.

Vitals serve as the foundational definition of success year over year. When paired with a set of strategic objectives, vitals targets define the vision of an organization. Measuring performance is difficult and imperfect. Through the development of vitals, organizations can drive continuous improvement through a culture of measurement and feedback.

Maybe the greatest value of strong organizational vitals emerges through their annual scrutiny for significance and measurement. Because all indicators are imperfect, they should be evaluated regularly for their ability to offer meaningful insight. When a vital no longer does this, it needs to be revised, overhauled, or scrapped altogether. Annually completing this process is not just a routine check; it's a strategic exercise that imbues teams with deeper clarity and strengthens their conviction in the pursuit of success. This cyclical process of reassessment and adaptation transforms vitals into a dynamic tool, creating a culture of continuous improvement and allowing teams to not just track but also actively influence the trajectory of the organization's success.

**Examples:**

- **Product Vitals:** Monthly Recurring Revenue (MRR), Lifetime Value (LTV)
- **People Vitals:** Engagement Score, Culture Index Score
- **Financial Vitals:** Sustainable Revenue, Profitability
- **Impact Vitals for Nonprofits:** Job Placements, Permanent Housing Placements

## Tenets: How Do We Work?

Here's an example of how tenets can guide can guide the ways team collaborate and work through tension:

While putting in long hours to prepare for a major event, Derrick noticed tension building within the team. As the final three weeks approached, an unexpected development arose, causing several team members, including Derrick, to work late hours. Derrick voiced his concern to the team, saying, "Mark is leading this effort, and I can't shake the feeling that better planning could've spared us this last-minute scramble."

Emily chimed in, "I understand where you're coming from. I share the frustration, but I wonder if there are factors at play that we're not aware of."

Recently, the team developed some organizational tenets, and they decided to use them to navigate the situation. Two tenets seemed particularly relevant:

1. Fearless Feedback: We foster an environment where feedback is seen as a gift, failures are viewed as learning opportunities, safety is prioritized, accountability is encouraged, and reflection is promoted.
2. Open Communication and Transparency: Maintain open and transparent communication channels to facilitate collaboration, feedback, and alignment of efforts toward common goals.

After considering both tenets, Derrick and Emily concluded that the best approach was to have an honest conversation with Mark about their perceptions and to try to understand his perspective.

## What are Tenets
Tenets are the three to five most important design principles about how work should work. They finish the sentence, "Our team works best when we _____."

## Why Tenets Matter
Tenets create a bridge between the other Identity components and the operational practices that bring them to life. They are the principles

that teams create together to ensure that their operating practices are aligned with their Identity. Many teams find the process of developing tenets liberating because they have never taken the time to claim how they want work to work.

Defining beliefs about what motivates people, how work gets done, and how to address issues can ensure teams work together in alignment with their Identity. Tenets inform and guide operational norms, strengthen team alignment, and help guide root cause analysis when tensions or issues arise. When activated, tenets enable a beliefs-centered organizational operating system.

Tenets offer a common language for teams to gain alignment about how work works. They clarify and elevate expectations, resulting in reduced stress and uncertainty around collaborative work. They guide how teams collaborate with the aim of strengthening team cohesion.

**Examples:**

- People are motivated by human connection, autonomy, and purpose.
- We embrace an internal culture that is entrepreneurial and growth-oriented in nature, encouraging an exploration of new ideas and learning through failure.
- People are motivated and engaged when they have clarity of expectation and focus.

# Smoke and Mirrors

As Sarah walked through the spacious, open-plan office on her first day at Catalyst Tech, she felt a surge of excitement. She had seen the ads promoting the company's positive culture, and now she saw similar posters on the walls. However, as the weeks turned into months, Sarah's initial enthusiasm began to wane. The once-inspiring quotes and values seemed to be just decorative elements, disconnected from the day-to-day realities of working at Catalyst Tech. In meetings, new ideas were often met with resistance, contrary to the company's proclaimed value of innovation. The inclusivity promoted in their mission statement did not match the distinct lack of diversity in leadership roles and an undercurrent of unspoken hierarchies.

The break room conversations often revolved around job dissatisfaction and the stark gap between the company's stated Identity and the reality of its workplace culture. It became clear to Sarah that Catalyst's beautifully articulated values, mission, and beliefs were more of a facade, a smokescreen that poorly veiled the true nature of the organization's environment.

Unfortunately, this scenario is far too common in organizations. Many workplaces present an appealing facade of values and beliefs but fail to embed these ideals into the fabric of their everyday operations and employee interactions. They create mission statements and value propositions that sound impressive but lack the substance and commitment to bring them to life. This superficiality leads to a culture where the stated Identity is merely a set of words on a website or a poster rather than a living, breathing ethos at the heart of the work that guides every decision, action, and interaction within the organization.

For an organization to embody its Identity, it must bring the Identity Lever to life, both by how it's defined—ideally through each of the six components discussed here—and by integrating Identity into its practices around people and systems.

# The Compass

Once a team has taken the time to clarify each of the six components of Identity, we recommend organizing them in a simple format to bring this Identity to life. **The Compass is a strategic orientation tool that captures the six essential components of Identity in an easy-to-digest format.** While many strategic plans are gathering dust on a shelf, the Compass is meant to be used and referenced. In addition to Identity, it includes a succinct, directional three-year vision.

The key to the Compass is that it's accessible to everyone and frequently referenced. Because of its lean format, it's easy to update as needed. At the heart of the Compass's value is clarity. By distilling an organization's most essential Identity and vision, the Compass serves as the ultimate tool to align and empower teams.

*Harvard Business Review* stated that 95% of employees are unaware of their 'company's vision and strategy. The consequences can be negative and far-reaching when employees do not understand and align with the overarching strategy of the organization. They include time wasted on nonessential work, financial loss due to inefficiencies, cultural and organizational health issues, employee disengagement, and much more. Without a strategic plan that is easy to understand and orient to, organizations are likely to have a significantly diluted impact.

Leaders need tools they can carry with them, apply in any situation, and use to onboard people easily. They need this Compass to orient them to the way, the why, and the how. **To be responsive to the dynamic, ever-changing world we live in, teams need tools that allow them to move quickly while still honoring their Identity and Vision.**

Of course, the Compass alone does not ensure your Identity and vision come to life, but that's where the other five Levers come into play, so keep reading.

Visit https://www.6levers.co/our-identity to see the 6 Levers Identity. It guides us in strategic and day-to-day decisions and informs the type of culture we want to build as we grow our company. It will do the same for you.

## Recap of the Identity Lever

The Identity Lever captures the soul of the organization: what it believes, why it exists, and what it values. A team with a strong Identity has clear beliefs, mission, Theory of Impact, values, vitals, and tenets, and they capture all of these components in an organizational Compass.

**Questions for Reflection**

1. Do you feel your organization has a strong Identity?
2. Can team members articulate how their work contributes or connects to the organization's Identity?
3. What can you do today to take one step toward clarifying your organization's Identity?
4. Out of all 6 Levers, does strengthening Identity feel like a Lever to focus on?

# Leadership

# Leadership

When Simon Sinek first told Harvard Business School professor Amy Cuddy about Barry-Wehmiller, she thought he was embellishing the story. She didn't believe what he described could exist. But when Amy and Simon visited the industrial manufacturing company in October 2014 to write a case study about it, she saw it for herself.

"It's like a little utopia," Amy shared in an interview during their visit.

Amy and Simon weren't there to learn about advanced machinery or industrial best practices. Instead, they visited to uncover the essence of what Barry-Wehmiller had become renowned for—a people-centered approach to workplace culture and leadership.

"What we witness here at Barry-Wehmiller is basically human beings the way they're supposed to be," Simon said. "Unfortunately, we view it as the exception. We view it as an outlier, but it's actually the way we're supposed to be. It's what makes us feel good and live longer and enjoy life."

During their visit, Cuddy and Sinek witnessed a remarkable corporate culture that transcended conventional business practices. Each employee was not just a cog in the machine but a valued individual, integral to the company's heart and soul. The ethos was clear: a workplace should be a sanctuary where everyone feels they matter, where their full potential is nurtured, and where they can return home feeling cared for and fulfilled.

This heightened focus on people was led by Bob Chapman, the visionary CEO, who, after a series of breakthroughs, moved the company toward what he called "Truly Human Leadership." Success was no longer measured by financials but by, as he said, "the way we touch the lives of people."

"I won't go to my grave proud of the machines I've built," Chapman said. "I'll be proud of the people we built—who we allowed to find their gifts, develop their gifts, and be appreciated for their gifts."

Chapman and his team realized that there could be no definition of success that didn't include thriving and engaged team members. Their story illustrates what is possible when fundamental human needs, such as the need for meaning and contribution, are met and what can happen when leaders understand that people are the heart of work. Putting this idea into practice to inform your system, identity, and priorities is what the Leadership Lever is all about. It's the Lever specifically designed to guide organizations to systematically harness the people component and develop leadership in all team members.

## People Are the Lifeblood

The transformative journey of Barry-Wehmiller underscores a universal principle—the vitality of a healthy organization is intricately tied to the well-being of its people. Bob Chapman grew to understand an idea critical to the success of any organization: **people are the heart of work.** While this isn't a new idea, the sad reality is that, according to Gallup, just one-third of employees are engaged. Much has been written about the connection between engagement and performance, but few organizations have created cultures that lead to high levels of sustained engagement.

Creating an engaged culture requires leaders to commit to center fundamental human needs and to build systems that support them. It becomes a shared journey where the success of individuals is inseparable from the success of the organization. The Leadership Lever puts this idea into practice, operationalizing the belief that people are the heart of work.

## It's Within All of Us

Equally as important as the belief that people are the heart of work is the belief that everyone is capable of embodying leadership. To cultivate an organization with higher engagement, we cannot relegate the tenets of great leadership to a select few in managerial positions—they must be recognized as capabilities inherent in every individual and, therefore, expected of everyone on the team.

In the journey of Barry-Wehmiller, this belief wasn't merely a theoretical concept but a guiding principle that shaped the fabric of their organizational culture. Chapman understood that true leadership extends beyond executive boardrooms. It thrives on the factory floor, in the offices, and within every team member's daily contributions.

Most leadership development courses and books are aimed at people in positions of authority: managers, supervisors, and executive teams. While people with positional authority do have incredible power to influence culture and their teams—and we'll spend time later in the chapter talking about them specifically— we believe it's a mistake to only focus leadership development efforts on these people. Leadership isn't a position—it's an action, and it's how we show up. It's best observed through an environment where each person, irrespective of their title or role, feels empowered to lead in their unique way. Leadership isn't about commanding authority but rather about collaborating with and inspiring others. This approach challenges the conventional notion of leadership, suggesting that titles and hierarchical structures don't define one's capacity for leadership. Instead, it emerges from a deep understanding that everyone has the potential to contribute meaningfully and influence positive change.

Organizations that recognize and tap into the leadership potential of every individual create a culture of collaboration, innovation, and continuous improvement. When everyone is encouraged to lead, the organization becomes a dynamic ecosystem, and diverse perspectives and talents converge to reach unseen levels where people are highly engaged. The culture that's created gives individuals the ability to decide to lead. Organizations create that culture when they have the fundamental belief that anyone can lead. The belief in each other reinforces leadership and makes it possible across the organization.

What does it look like when everyone embraces leadership? We've identified four highly impactful practices anyone can use in their day-to-day work to activate the Leadership Lever and bring work to life—and life to work.

# Essential Leader Practices

Leadership, often misconstrued as only being about guiding others, starts with how we lead ourselves. Irrespective of one's formal position within an organization, each person possesses the inherent capacity for leadership. It is a journey that starts with personal development—a recognition that the most influential leadership begins from within. In a complex, modern workplace, self-leadership is critical. Before we can inspire and guide others, we must first be willing to dive into self-discovery and intentional growth. The four leader practices are a great place to start for anyone who wants to show up as a more intentional leader for their team.

These practices are behaviors anyone can call on at any moment. When a challenge arises, a team member can apply each of them to help navigate the situation with intentionality and mindfulness.

> **Essential Leader Practices**
>
> 1. **Curiosity:** The practice of continuous learning, carrying an open mind, and embracing new possibilities and perspectives
> 2. **Support/Challenge:** The ability to be understanding and highly supportive while also holding high expectations and challenging one to do their best work
> 3. **Self-Awareness:** The intentional way we regularly seek to learn more about ourselves and how we are seen
> 4. **Vulnerability:** Having the courage to be our true self at work, even through risk and uncertainty

# Curiosity

During her early days as a PhD student, Amy Edmondson had a hypothesis about the relationship between the quality of teamwork and medical errors. However, when confronted with the stark reality that the data seemed to reveal the exact opposite of what she expected, she was struck with anxiety. Somehow, the data revealed higher rates of error among the highest-performing teams. She faced a wave of disappointment and anxiety, questioning the implications for her early career. After all her hard work, she wondered if she would have to come up with a completely new line of theory to study.

Despite the setback, Edmondson's curiosity shone through. Rather than give in to defeat, she posed a daring new question: What if the seemingly superior teams weren't making fewer mistakes but rather were more transparent about acknowledging them? This insightful wondering led her to a new realization: the ease with which errors could be concealed. Perhaps the hallmark of high-performing teams lay not in their flawless execution but in their culture of openness and accountability to each other.

This newfound curiosity ignited a series of subsequent studies delving deeper into the role of psychological safety in fostering resilient teams. The ripple effects of her groundbreaking research were profound, with the concept of psychological safety now firmly ingrained in our understanding of cohesive team dynamics.

In the face of adversity and uncertainty, Edmondson's relentless curiosity changed the way we think about the importance of psychological safety in the workplace. Her willingness to be curious has left a measurable mark on the landscape of employee engagement, shaping the way we perceive and cultivate effective teamwork. Without her continued inquiry and open-mindedness, we wouldn't have the gift of understanding the important connection between psychological safety and cohesive teams.

### What does Curiosity look like?

A leader who:
- Is always learning and seeking new information and experiences
- Seeks creative solutions to tough situations
- Wonders why and explores novel possibilities
- Defaults to a "beginner's mind"
- Appreciates new perspectives
- Recognizes their limited view and accepts that they don't have all the answers
- Raises big questions and challenges the standard way of thinking

In the face of uncertainty and adversity, the curious leader approaches challenges with an openness and a sense of wonder. They help those around them to be more curious, as well, because curiosity tends to be contagious. When teams embrace this leader practice, it fundamentally shifts their ability to effectively problem-solve. By creating the space to go upstream to diagnose an issue, they are more likely to get to the root. Curiosity leads to more productive solutions and innovation. This approach challenges conventional wisdom, encourages the exploration of overlooked questions, and transforms the discomfort of uncertainty into fertile ground for growth.

**By creating a culture of inquiry and experimentation, the curious leader inspires those around them to think critically, explore boldly, and challenge the status quo.** They recognize the value of humility, acknowledging their own limitations and embracing the diverse insights of others.

## Support/Challenge

DeMeco Ryans, head coach of the Houston Texans, is acclaimed for his relatable demeanor, high energy, and demanding yet supportive coaching style. He exemplifies the essence of Support/Challenge leadership. His players regard him as the "most amazing teacher ever," illustrating his knack for building a culture where individuals willingly give their all.

Ryans doesn't dictate standards but instead emphasizes upholding those set by his players. As he aptly puts it, "We have a standard ... our guys set that standard." His approach is rooted in understanding each player, knowing when to push and when to back off. "You have to understand the people you're working with. That's how you know when you can push," he affirms.

He navigates the delicate balance between pushing and uplifting his players, recognizing that effective leadership entails understanding individual personalities and motivations. "How I talk to one guy is not how I can talk to others," he remarks, showcasing his adaptability.

Ryans's leadership style underscores the vital role of meaningful support coupled with high expectations and accountability. He emphasizes, "It's all about finding that right balance."

It's no surprise that he led the Houston Texans to the playoffs in his first year as a head coach. This was quite the feat, considering most experts picked them to be one of the worst teams in the league. Those who know him well weren't surprised. He has the ability to bring out the best of his players, like few coaches can.

## What does Support/Challenge look like?

**A leader who:**

**Supports:**

- Encourages and instills belief and confidence
- Has empathy and seeks to understand
- Offers tangible help and coaching
- Recognizes effort and achievement
- Is responsive and adaptive to individual needs

**Challenges:**

- Believes in individuals' potential and calling them to be their best
- Consistently sets clear and high expectations
- Holds people accountable
- Challenges individuals to find solutions and make progress
- Thoughtfully encourages individuals to step outside their comfort zones

In essence, DeMeco Ryans showcases how effective leadership hinges on the ability to blend meaningful support with unwavering challenge. By understanding his players and striking the right balance between the two, he creates an environment where individuals thrive, grow, and surpass their limitations.

**Support/Challenge leadership embodies the ability to provide warmth, understanding, and meaningful support while simultaneously setting high expectations and fostering accountability.** It's about creating an environment where individuals feel encouraged to excel while they are also being held to their highest standards of performance.

## Self-Awareness

A self-aware leader possesses a deep understanding of their own strengths, weaknesses, emotions, and values. They have a keen awareness of how their behaviors and decisions impact those around them, allowing them to communicate effectively, build trust, and navigate conflicts constructively. Self-aware leaders are open to feedback and continuously seek opportunities for personal growth and development. They lead with authenticity and empathy, inspiring their teams to reach their full potential while fostering a culture of transparency and mutual respect.

> ### What does Self-Awareness look like?
>
> A leader who:
> - Understands how their words and actions impact others and behaves with clear communication and emotional intelligence
> - Builds trust and rapport with their team members
> - Is open to feedback, adapts their leadership style, and continuously learns and grows

Becoming more self-aware as a leader involves a deliberate effort to seek and process feedback. One crucial aspect is understanding the significance of feedback from the right sources. It's not merely about asking for feedback but also being discerning about who you seek feedback from. This requires identifying individuals who can offer constructive criticism and valuable insights within an environment of trust. In her book *Insight: Why We're Not as Self-Aware as We Think, and How Seeing Ourselves Clearly Helps Us Succeed at Work and in Life*, Tasha Eurich defines "loving critics" as people who genuinely care about your growth and are willing to provide honest feedback in a supportive manner. By focusing on feedback from these sources, leaders can gain deeper insights into their strengths, weaknesses, and areas for improvement.

Leaders can enhance their self-awareness by distinguishing between internal and external self-awareness, as outlined by Eurich. Internal self-awareness involves introspection, reflection, and understanding one's thoughts, emotions, and values. External self-awareness, on the other hand, pertains to how others perceive and experience you. By cultivating both internal and external self-awareness, leaders can develop a more holistic understanding of themselves and their impact on others. This dual focus enables leaders to align their self-perception with external perceptions, bridging potential gaps and fostering greater authenticity in their leadership approach.

Additionally, leaders can refine their approach to seeking feedback by narrowing the focus of their inquiries. Rather than asking for general feedback, they can be specific about the aspects they seek input on. This clarity helps to elicit more meaningful responses and actionable insights. By articulating specific areas for feedback, leaders can engage in more targeted self-reflection and development efforts, ultimately enhancing their self-awareness and effectiveness as leaders. Thus, by being intentional about feedback, discerning about its sources, and refining their approach, leaders can become increasingly self-aware.

## Vulnerability

Ever since Brené Brown's TED Talk on "The Power of Vulnerability," significant attention has been given to vulnerability in the workplace, particularly its role in fostering trust within teams. Despite this, many leaders struggle to understand the practical implementation of vulnerability. It's not merely about openly sharing vulnerabilities but about progressively sharing more while navigating the inherent risks, all while maintaining a sense of confidence and hopefulness. Practicing vulnerability with purpose is crucial; its aim should be centered around being authentic, building trust, strengthening psychological safety, and nurturing an atmosphere where teams can thrive.

In Jacob Morgan's book *Leading with Vulnerability: Unlock Your Greatest Superpower to Transform Yourself, Your Team, and Your Organization*, he underscores the importance of integrating vulnerability into the practice of leadership. An illustrative example involves reframing how leaders can effectively address their mistakes. Instead of merely apologizing for errors, leaders should openly discuss what they've learned from these experiences and articulate their plans for improvement. This more thoughtful use of vulnerability is what cultivates deeper connections with those we work with and makes it safer and more likely for others on the team to effectively bring vulnerability as well.

There may be no better place to look than Google to understand just how powerful it can be when a team creates a culture of vulnerability. In the tech giant's heavily referenced Project Aristotle, they found that the most influential quality of high-performing teams was psychological safety, or the degree to which a team believed it was safe to take risks, make mistakes, and be vulnerable. When we can rely on our teammates to offer support rather than judgment in moments of vulnerability, we unlock the full potential of collaboration, innovation, and resilience, creating a workspace where we are free to explore and grow while also striving to contribute our best.

### What does Vulnerability look like?

**A leader who:**
- Is accountable and admits their mistakes in front of the team
- Models humility by asking for help
- Shares why if they change their mind or course
- Leans into listening and is slow to speak
- Understands the relationship between vulnerability and building trust
- Understands that vulnerability needs to be practiced at all levels
- Shares just enough but doesn't overshare

Vulnerable leadership extends beyond admitting faults; it entails demonstrating a commitment to personal growth and development. When leaders transparently communicate the learnings and insights they gained from making mistakes, they instill a sense of dependability within their teams. Conversely, if leaders merely acknowledge their mistakes without showcasing a proactive approach to learning and growth, it can undermine the team's trust and cohesion, hindering their ability to depend on one another.

In essence, embracing vulnerability as a leadership practice is not about indiscriminately sharing vulnerabilities but about sharing with intent and purpose. By integrating vulnerability into their leadership style, leaders can foster trust, encourage experimentation, and create an environment where teams feel empowered to learn, grow, and succeed together.

◆ ◆ ◆

When teams embrace the four Essential Leader Practices and put them to use regularly, they create a common language to talk about what effective leadership looks like. This unlocks development opportunities, clarifies the practices that teams come to expect of each other, and has the potential to become a team's superpower. Imagine if every team in every organization had a leader like this. We would be looking at a different workforce—and a different society. These practices help to create the kind of leadership we need to navigate modern times.

# Leading Strategically in Today's World

The world has changed dramatically in the last couple of decades, from the increasing influence of social media to rapid technological changes, from the COVID-19 pandemic to the introduction of AI into everyday life, and from social turmoil to political turbulence that affects our workplaces. As the broader societal context changes, so does what it takes to be an effective leader.

Many of us experience a gap between what we learned makes a successful leader and what is required today in an increasingly dynamic and complex world. The key question for a leader used to be, "What do I hypothesize will be the best strategy for our team to accomplish our goals, and how do I get buy-in and manage people to reach those goals?" Now, success in the modern age requires a different question: "How do I create the conditions that promote organizational adaptability and the systems that enable it, high levels of engagement, and productive collaboration?" As we covered in Chapter 1, leading strategically in the modern world starts with moving upstream.

## Move Upstream

Many forces push us to live in a state of reactivity, putting out fires and operating downstream. When we have the curiosity and courage to go upstream, we can prevent problems from occurring in the first place.

When we focus downstream, we tend to only look at surface-level issues. We often want to blame a person for a problematic situation, but a person's behavior is only one of many influencing factors impacting a situation. When you encounter a "people problem," use it as a signal to go upstream to determine if it is just an individual performance issue or if a system issue needs to be addressed.

| Downstream | Upstream |
| --- | --- |
| Writing performance improvement plans | Proactively developing people through regular coaching |
| Mediating conflict between members of your team | Creating avenues for tension to regularly surface so conflict isn't as likely to become significant |
| Dealing with customer complaints due to overwork and poor quality | Having a better system for prioritization, leading to higher-quality work |

## Facilitate Alignment

According to research and consulting firm Gartner, "Half of change initiatives fail, and only 34% are a clear success. Lack of buy-in is a key success factor." The term "buy-in" has gained momentum in leadership circles in recent memory. But what leaders need is true alignment.

Oftentimes, leaders use a "Describe and Defend" approach to change, whereby a leader develops an idea and then tries to sell it to others. They think of potential objections and come up with defenses against them. The result is that employees may comply but not buy in, which leads to implementation challenges and power struggles.

The alternative approach to change is called "Propose and Experiment." In this approach, leaders bring people into the problem and facilitate idea generation. They may bring a proposal or invite others to bring a proposal to the team. Team members are encouraged to surface concerns to make the proposal better.

When we shift from the "Describe and Defend" approach to the "Propose and Experiment" approach to change, we create a culture of collaboration, innovation, and genuine buy-in, increasing the likelihood of successful and sustainable organizational change. It's one thing to have initial alignment from the team; it's another to be committed to learning and changing course quickly as reality unfolds. This is the Leadership Lever in action.

## Learn and Adapt

To succeed in today's dynamic environments, teams must become what Peter Senge has coined "learning organizations," where people are encouraged to take calculated risks and explore new ideas. In these organizations, failure is seen as an opportunity for learning and improvement.

The learning organization has characteristics that any leader can embrace and implement.

- Experimentation: The organization values experimentation, and failures are treated as opportunities for learning and improvement rather than reasons for blame and punishment.
- Feedback: Teams actively seek feedback from customers, employees, and stakeholders to improve processes and products or services.
- Adaptation: Teams implement formal processes to capture and document lessons learned from both successes and failures, and they adapt strategies in response to what they learn.
- Leadership Modeling: The leadership team demonstrates a commitment to continuous learning and personal development.

# Embrace Management as Leadership

Leadership is not reserved for people in management positions. When leadership is thriving on a team, it's because many team members—if not all—are contributing to it. However, managers still carry an outsized influence on teams. Gallup reports that managers account for 70% of the variance in employee engagement scores on teams.

> **3 Ways to Manage as a Leader**
> 1. Build team psychological safety
> 2. Understand human fundamental needs.
> 3. Lead like a coach.

While managers aren't solely responsible for a culture of leadership, they have more influence than any other person on the team. Because of this, it would be extremely challenging for any team to realize sustained health if the manager wasn't committed to intentionally developing their own leadership capabilities. Managers can embrace a handful of practices to help their teams go upstream and achieve greater alignment and adaptability.

# Building Team Psychological Safety

As we'll discuss in the Cohesion chapter, team psychological safety is the most important aspect of high-performing teams. Because of managers' outsized influence, it's critical for them to actively work to build a culture of trust rooted in team psychological safety. A great place for team leaders to begin is to become more aware of the behaviors that build and break psychological safety. Here we outlined a few key dimensions to consider, along with a few examples of behaviors that build and break psychological safety.

### Dimension: Our Disposition

| Builders | Breakers |
| --- | --- |
| Shares relevant personal experiences to connect on a human level | Keeps conversations strictly business without personal touchpoints |
| Brings a sense of warmth and positivity | Displays closed body language, such as crossed arms or avoiding eye contact |

### Dimension: How We Respond

| Builders | Breakers |
| --- | --- |
| When someone shares difficult news, leaders (1) pause, (2) say thank you, and (3) focus questions on the future (e.g., How can we make things right?) | Reacts defensively to feedback, concerns, or opposing opinions |
| Asks clarifying questions to understand different perspectives | Ignores or sidesteps difficult conversations |

### Dimension: Our Humility

**Builders**

Admits mistakes and shares lessons learned from them

Shows appreciation for others' strengths and contributions

**Breakers**

Rarely demonstrates vulnerability

Downplays or ignores the contributions of others

---

As leaders, it's important for us to recognize that many of our behaviors are either building or breaking psychological safety. Trying to foster engagement without developing team psychological safety is like pressing the accelerator without first releasing the brake. When team members do not feel comfortable expressing themselves, critical information about the organization is lost, and employee engagement and organizational performance suffer. By intentionally adopting behaviors that build trust—such as sharing personal experiences, responding thoughtfully to feedback, and showing humility—leaders can create a supportive atmosphere that promotes trust.

# Understanding Fundamental Human Needs

One of the most impactful shifts a leader can make is the intentional effort to understand the unique needs of team members and work deliberately to meet them. Within any team lie fundamental human needs—crucial elements that, when fulfilled, unlock many positive outcomes. These needs encompass dimensions such as meaning, contribution, belonging, clarity, growth, and autonomy, forming the bedrock of a thriving and engaged team.

While everyone shares these needs, their significance varies from person to person. Autonomy might be critical for some, while others find a deep sense of fulfillment in belonging. A leader can intentionally develop their skills to discern these individual nuances, understanding that a one-size-fits-all approach falls short in unlocking engagement.

Consider the scenario of a team member grappling with persistent challenges in meeting project deadlines. A leader faces a choice: they could attempt to persuade the individual of the project's significance and the collective impact of success. Alternatively, they could delve deeper, seeking to understand the unmet needs that might underlie the performance struggles.

By embarking on the latter path, the leader might uncover that the team member's need for contribution isn't being met. Perhaps, in the maze of tasks, the team member struggles to see the direct connection between their work and the broader project goals. This understanding reframes the leader's approach from a focus merely on project importance to addressing the individual's need for a meaningful contribution.

Leaders who commit to understanding the diverse needs of their team can then proactively shape the working conditions that facilitate meeting those needs. This isn't a generic prescription but a tailored strategy that acknowledges the individuality within the team. The result is a positive feedback loop—meeting individual needs sparks positive emotions, which, in turn, drive behaviors that enhance the collective well-being of the team.

Most significantly, this approach becomes a potent antidote to the prevalent issue of disengagement that plagues many teams. By aligning leadership efforts with the diverse needs of team members, a leader has the power not only to unlock engagement but also to reverse the negative trends that often lead to mass disengagement. This commitment to understanding and meeting the needs of the team creates the potential of a culture where individuals flourish, teams thrive, and engagement is higher than ever.

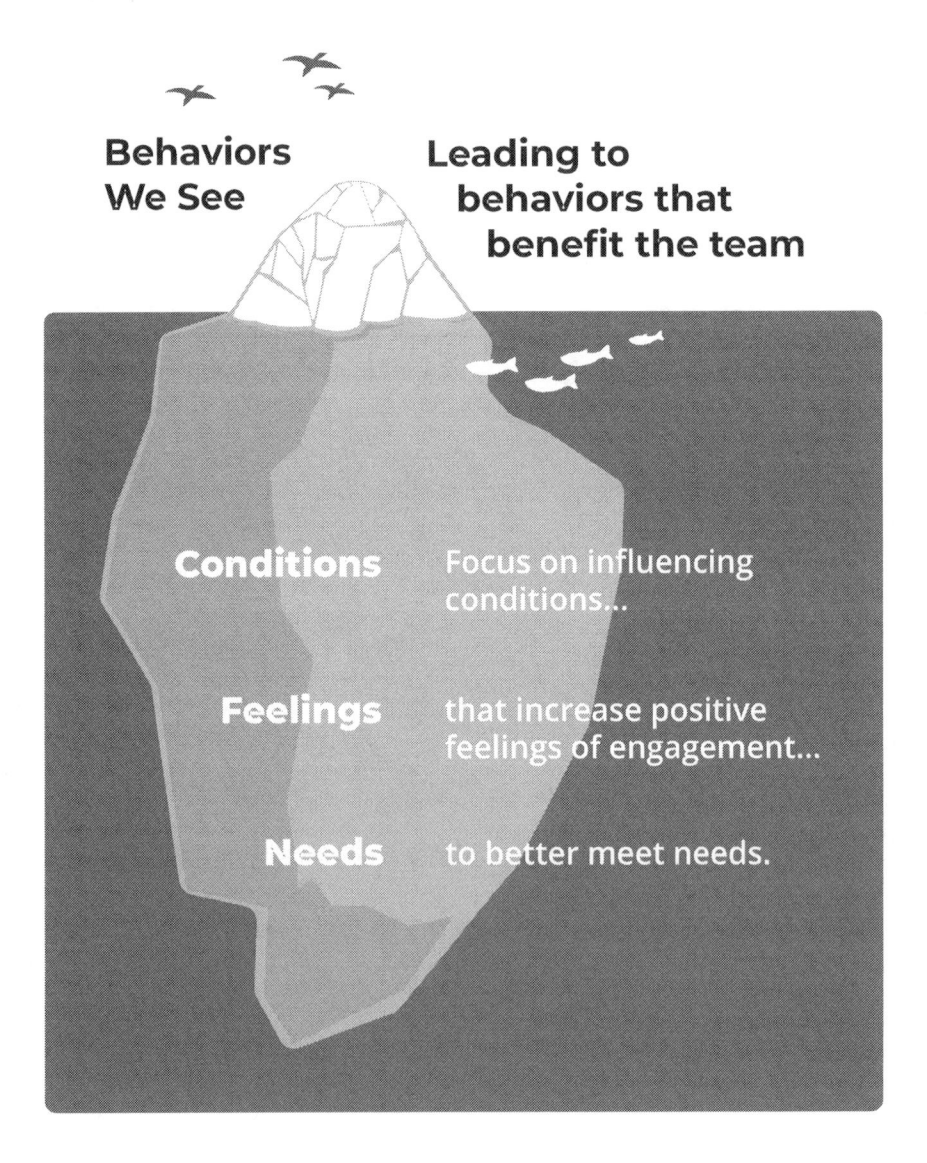

**Behaviors We See**

**Leading to behaviors that benefit the team**

**Conditions** — Focus on influencing conditions...

**Feelings** — that increase positive feelings of engagement...

**Needs** — to better meet needs.

# Lead Like a Coach

Modern leadership often demands approaches that might not have been modeled for us. One of the biggest departures from traditional management styles is when leaders embrace the role of coach. We define coaching as the art of helping individuals unlock their own potential and discover solutions, primarily through attentive listening and thought-provoking questions that instill new insights and confidence.

Many of us have encountered managers who tended toward directive guidance rather than creating a space for learning and discovery. Adopting a coaching approach in leadership is pivotal for enhancing both the performance and the personal development of employees. Beyond that, it nurtures a culture of empowerment where team members are inspired to experiment, collaborate, and actively contribute to finding innovative solutions. The coaching philosophy encourages individuals to recognize the extent of their capabilities, largely because of the safety offered to explore and grow.

An effective coaching style requires active listening, even over insightful questions and certainly over offering advice. This often-overlooked leadership skill plays a crucial role in facilitating positive growth in individuals. Managers who excel in listening make employees more self-aware of their strengths and weaknesses, more open to diverse perspectives, and more inclined to collaborate rather than compete with colleagues.

Following listening, the next critical skill in leading like a coach is the ability to ask good questions—an art few leaders take the time to explore. 'Various historical figures have been credited with saying wise words like these, and they're worth repeating here: "If I had an hour to solve a problem, I'd spend fifty-five minutes thinking about the problem and asking questions and five minutes thinking about solutions."

Well-crafted questions possess the transformative power to encourage reflection, foster meaningful dialogue leading to new insights, get to the heart of the matter, and inspire action.

As you delve into the art of asking better questions, consider the following guide:

- Use open questions to open dialogue: Open-ended inquiries invite exploration and thoughtful responses, encouraging a more profound exchange of ideas.
- Avoid "why" questions to sidestep defensiveness: Steering clear of "'why'" questions helps create a non-confrontational atmosphere, fostering a more constructive dialogue.
- Watch for leading questions that direct the conversation: Be mindful of inadvertently influencing responses with leading questions and instead allow the conversation to unfold naturally.
- Consider the order of questions in a coaching conversation: Sequencing questions thoughtfully contributes to the flow of the discussion, ensuring a purposeful exploration of ideas and solutions.

Our colleague, Jo Pang, created this simple visual to help leaders understand the value of listening and asking more than advising.

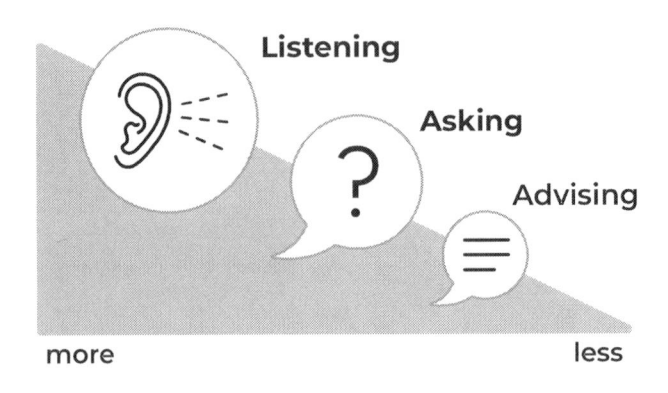

**Listening**

**Asking**

**Advising**

more                                    less

# Leadership Creates More Leadership

By embracing leadership as an inherent capability within everyone, organizations can cultivate a culture of collaboration, adaptability, and deeper engagement. This shift challenges traditional ideas about leadership, emphasizing that leadership is defined not by titles but by actions and attitudes. Barry-Wehmiller's journey underscores this belief, demonstrating that true leadership flourishes not only among managers but among everyone when organizations bring intention to meeting human needs. Even in the healthiest systems, intentional leadership is still required to build thriving, engaged teams. Keeping people at the heart of work will go a long way in creating a culture where it's possible for anyone to bring great leadership.

### Recap of the Leadership Lever

The Leadership Lever offers the tools, practices, and mindsets needed to build a culture of Leadership. A team with a strong culture of Leadership recognizes and develops the Leadership potential of every individual, and it has tools and practices to develop these skills.

**Questions for Reflection**

1. Have you clarified the leader practices and characteristics you hope to see in your organization?

2. Does your organization have an approach to intentionally develop leaders?

3. Out of all 6 Levers, does strengthening Leadership seem like one of the priorities for your organization?

# LEADERSHIP

# Focus

# Focus

We live in a world rife with distractions. We're bombarded with information from all angles in various forms, many coming directly from the small supercomputers most of us carry in our pockets. We were already struggling to discern what is most important, and now we have even more information to wade through. As we constantly receive news about threats and opportunities, it's even harder to commit to the priorities we set for ourselves and our work. That's why leaders need the Focus Lever.

Despite the various tech tools that have popped up to help us manage this information overwhelm, most leaders still struggle with focus. It's not just about one's attention span or ability to concentrate from one minute to the next. It's about too many priorities competing for attention and the fight to maintain focus on the most important work over weeks, months, and even years.

It's a struggle for leaders as individuals (how to manage personal workload), and it's an even greater struggle for teams. If a team is not aligned on what is most important, then each individual member is deciding for themselves, pulling the team's collective attention in a different direction and compounding the effects of not focusing on the right things.

As the number of people on a team increases, the number of connection points increases exponentially. If each person has a different understanding of what's most important or is pulling in a different direction, the opportunity for chaos increases exponentially as well.

A Deloitte survey found that, "Nearly half of the survey respondents say their organization's leaders are struggling to identify what to prioritize because they are overwhelmed by the number and frequency of disruptive shifts occurring." The Focus Lever is all about setting priorities as well as creating a team culture that supports Focus.

Struggles around Focus sound like this:

- "I'm constantly putting out fires, trapped in the tyranny of the urgent, with no room to focus on what matters most."
- "It's like drinking from a fire hose—my to-do list is overwhelming, and everything feels equally urgent, making it hard to accomplish anything meaningful."
- "Misalignment with my manager over priorities leaves me uncertain and unconfident about achieving our big annual goals."

Underlying these struggles are three major challenges when it comes to Focus: an unclear process to set priorities, no process to monitor priorities, and no system to adjust priorities. Let's go over these challenges one by one.

## Unclear Process to Set Priorities

Teams can have any number of answers to how they decide what to focus on. Some teams don't set priorities at all, which leads to each individual determining on their own what is most important, with no shared objectives. Other teams have way too many priorities and struggle to juggle them all. Yet other teams have a system, but it's insufficient or ineffective.

Common problems people experience when setting priorities include:

1. Lack of agency: Individuals don't have input on their team's priorities, and instead, priorities are handed down from a leader or separate leadership team. Team members feel they don't have autonomy or ownership in carrying out priorities.
2. Lack of meaning: The team doesn't see the meaning or impact of their 'priorities.

3. Lack of clarity: There's no framework to set priorities, or the framework changes too often. This can result in too many priorities or priorities that can't be measured.
4. Unrealistic understanding of capacity: The team gets excited by the possibilities, but members are blind to the capacity these efforts will take. They end up committing to priorities they can't possibly accomplish and then feel like they failed.

## No Process to Monitor Priorities

The work doesn't end with setting priorities. That's just the beginning. Most teams lack the discipline to sustain their focus on the priorities they set for themselves. No matter the horizon—annual, quarterly, or even weekly—continuing to prioritize what your team has deliberately defined as most important is surprisingly difficult. It's common for a team to take the time to set priorities at the beginning of a quarter and then forget about them until it's time to set the next round. Once they've repeated this pattern a few times, teams often drop the process altogether, believing it to be unnecessary.

This phenomenon is often due to a lack of tools, strategies, and rhythms to keep the priorities alive. Staying focused on priorities doesn't happen by accident. Teams that establish a Rhythm and thoughtful protocol to monitor their Focus are better equipped to keep these priorities top of mind. The Rhythm Lever contains powerful tools to help sustain Focus, and we'll cover those in the Rhythm chapter.

## No System to Adjust Priorities

Conventional wisdom suggests Focus is about deciding on goals and sticking to them, no matter what. But "effective priorities" does not mean "set in stone." It's a problem if priorities change constantly, but it's also a problem if priorities never change or adapt in response to emergent work, challenges, opportunities, or ideas. The problem arises when there's no system or agreement on how to handle these inevitable urgent needs.

When a brilliant idea, urgent task or fire, or exciting opportunity emerges as a threat to your focus, rather than throwing current priorities out the window, consider how to respond methodically and intentionally in an agreed-upon way to recalibrate your Focus. A team's ability to reestablish and recommit to its Focus when it comes under threat is the keystone that holds Focus together.

◆ ◆ ◆

Creating clear Focus is a challenge for many teams. But it's also incredibly important. The Focus Lever equips teams with tools and practices to align on their biggest priorities—what matters most. Beyond these tools and strategies for capturing and maintaining Focus, this Lever is also about creating a culture of Focus where the team believes in it, respects it, and honors its importance. Achieving strong Focus requires tools and team commitment, often in the form of tenets (see the guidance about creating tenets in the Identity Lever chapter).

# Why Focus Matters

Focus—or a lack of Focus—has an incredible impact on an organization, from the top to the bottom and from the big picture to the day-to-day. It affects how individuals work together, how teams work together, and how the organization functions at the highest level. A strong Focus Lever is critical for several reasons.

**Strong Focus**

- Is freeing
- Unlocks innovation
- Enhances well-being and engagement

## Focus Is Freeing

It's counterintuitive, but true. When you develop clear Focus, it frees you to do your best work.

The default for many leaders is to say "yes" to everything. We want to be helpful to our teams. We want to be a "team player." We want to be visionary and embrace new opportunities. We fall victim to the tendency to overestimate what we can accomplish in a week or year.

The unfortunate truth is that our resources are limited. Even if money is plentiful, we only have so many hours in a day, so much attention, and so much energy. When our "yes" outpaces our available resources, we end up stretched too thin and unable to deliver excellence. It happens at the individual level, at the team level, and at the organization level.

We cannot accomplish everything, so it's critical to identify what is most important and focus our energy there. This requires admitting that not everything is equally important and only a few things matter most.

This idea is called "essentialism," and it came from the book *Essentialism: The Disciplined Pursuit of Less* by Greg McKeown. By embracing essentialism, leaders and teams can identify and prioritize the essential activities that align with the organization's strategic goals while eliminating nonessential distractions and tasks that hinder progress and dilute impact.

Once we admit that only a few things matter, we must be disciplined and rigorous about saying "no" to what is not most important.

When we have a clear answer to "What is most important to your team right now?" it frees us to say "no" or "not yet" to opportunities outside of our Focus.

We are free to:

- give our "yes" all our resources
- do our best work, which in turn energizes us; no one likes to underperform

We are free from:

- the burden of being overworked and overstretched
- delivering poor work because we didn't have time to deliver excellence

Strong Focus is all about identifying what matters most and channeling the best resources there. **By intentionally choosing what matters most and saying "no" to the rest, you are free to invest your time and energy in the work that matters most to you and your team.** We all want to feel that our work matters. Learning to say "no" can help.

Easier said than done, right?

## Focus Unlocks Innovation

The legendary stories from the world of business usually revolve around what a leader does. But sometimes, the most incredible successes come from what a leader stops doing.

When Steve Jobs returned to Apple in 1997, the company was not in great shape. Fresh off its worst-ever financial quarter, its market share was in decline, its structure was disorganized, and its product lineup was bloated. Jobs realized he needed to bring focus to Apple's strategy and operations, starting with getting rid of underperforming projects to focus more resources on what he believed would be the winners.

Many in the industry were shocked when Jobs narrowed the product lineup to only four products: the iMac, PowerBook, Power Mac, and PowerBook Duo. By eliminating nonessential products and focusing on a smaller, more refined portfolio, Apple could concentrate its resources and deliver products of exceptional quality. This focus on simplicity and excellence became a defining characteristic of Apple's brand.

Jobs also elevated the importance of design and user experience, recognizing that these aspects would set Apple apart from its competitors. He famously stated, "Design is not just what it looks like and feels like. Design is how it works." This focus on design and user experience was instrumental in the success of products like the iMac, iPod, iPhone, and later the iPad.

Through his unwavering focus on essential products, exceptional design, and the customer experience, Jobs turned Apple into one of the most successful companies in the world. He brought incredible focus to Apple, and he also had the courage and foresight to stop doing activities outside of that core focus.

His ability to cut through the noise, prioritize the essentials, and concentrate the company's efforts on a few key areas demonstrated the power of focus in driving innovation, revitalizing a struggling business, and transforming an industry.

**Focus drives collaboration and innovation.** When teams are clear about their biggest goals, it empowers them to take ownership of their collective priorities. Using a results-based goal-setting framework spurs innovation because it allows teams to come up with creative ways to achieve the result. A leader of a front-line service organization explained it this way: "I give my team the drawing, but it's up to them to figure out how to color in the picture."

When we talk about Focus helping leaders find more time, this is part of the reason. When teams have clear direction and can exercise autonomy and creativity to achieve that direction, it frees the leader from the burden of trying to do it alone. With clear Focus, a collection of individuals can work as a team.

**Focus unlocks creativity and breakthrough thinking by creating the mental space for deep work and exploration.**

## Focus Enhances Well-Being and Engagement

When a team is not clear on its top-line priorities or the goals shift too often, it has a demotivating effect on the team members because it fails to meet the employees' fundamental needs. Focus is not merely about operational challenges—it is one of the most important areas to get right to ensure you're meeting team members' needs at work.

Let's look at three of those fundamental human needs that underlie many of the challenges with Focus:

1. Agency: We all need to have a sense of control and input in the decisions that affect our work. When priorities are dictated from above without considering the perspectives and expertise of the team, it can lead to feelings of disempowerment and disconnection.
2. Meaning: We crave a sense of purpose and a clear understanding of how our efforts contribute to the larger goals and vision of the organization. When team members can't see the meaning or impact of their priorities, they may struggle to find motivation and engagement in their work.
3. Clarity: Clarity is essential to provide a sense of structure and direction. We are wired to seek order and organization, and constantly shifting goals or a lack of clear priorities can lead to confusion and frustration. This, in turn, can result in too many priorities or priorities that cannot be effectively measured, further exacerbating the problem.

**When leaders connect priority setting to fundamental human needs such as agency, meaning, and clarity, they can create a culture that fosters engagement and motivation in their teams.** Because unmet human needs at work can lead to disengagement, setting and pursuing priorities isn't solely about operational efficiency but also about fulfilling these core human desires.

# What Focus Looks Like

A set of clear and meaningful goals is only part of the picture of a strong Focus. Focus appears on various levels throughout the organization.

- It's a mindset. Focus is an ethos, a core tenet guiding how teams work. Teams need to champion tenets that give them permission to pursue focused priorities.
- It's a process. Focus begins with big-picture clarity for the entire organization and continues with goal-setting frameworks throughout each team.
- It's a practice. No one is perfect at Focus right out of the gate. The real goal is to learn and progress, even more so than hitting a specific target.

This multi-level Focus looks like a meeting where team members ask, "How will this impact our capacity?" "What are the tradeoffs?" "How does this align to our mission and our quarterly priorities?" It looks like teams equipped with the tools and frameworks to set, monitor, and effectively adapt their Focus like clockwork. It looks like a culture that is comfortable with people saying "no."

Focus can take on a variety of forms, as well.

- Team: All types of teams at every level of an organization can create Focus, from a team of frontline workers to an organization-wide set of goals.
- Horizon: Focus happens across multiple time periods, from long-term (three- to five-year) to annual, semi-annual, weekly, or even daily.
- Format: Focus includes goal-setting, but it can also take the form of vitals targets and Agreements.

The idea of an organization having a strong Focus is more than a clear and meaningful set of goals—it's an ethos, a standard, or core tenet for operating. It's cultural. It begins with clear and meaningful three- and one-year organizational goals and continues with clear and meaningful goals at all levels and teams throughout the organization. But it's also the championing of core tenets related to Focus that are lived out every day. It's a culture comfortable with people saying "no" because they are so clear about what they have said "yes" to.

## The Focus Equation

One way teams can begin improving their Focus in a practical way is to adopt the Focus Equation. The equation is simply Vitals Targets + Priorities at any given time horizon. Teams should begin this process by first setting targets for each vital. Once those targets are set, they can move on to setting the unique priorities for whichever horizon they are planning. It works particularly well at both the annual and quarterly horizons, bringing a thematic focus to a year and a more narrow focus to a quarter. Let's look at an example of a team that is applying the Focus Equation at the quarterly horizon.

$$\text{Quarterly Vitals Targets} + \text{Quarterly Priorities} = \textbf{Quarterly Focus}$$

**Quarterly Vitals Targets:** The team begins with setting quarterly targets based on their annual vitals targets

**Quarterly Priorities:** The team then drafts quarter goals.

They first reflect on the previous quarter, pulling up the data to see what went well and what could have gone better in pursuit of hitting their targets. They then move on to reviewing their annual vitals targets.

They review both time horizons in an effort to understand how they are tracking toward their short-term and longer-term targets.

Reviewing both helps them begin to discern how to set their targets for the next quarter. The most important goal of reviewing data like this is to learn as a team. Reviewing the metrics should prompt authentically curious conversations rooted in a desire to learn and grow. Below is an example of a scorecard a team could review to help inform their discussion.

## Team Score Card

| Vital | Vital Definition | Annual Target | Q1 Vital Target |
|---|---|---|---|
| Employee engagement | % on Gallup Q12 survey | 65% | 61% |
| Revenue | Total gross revenue | $5 million | $2.5 million |
| Team health | Average 6 Levers Org Health Assessment score across all teams | 78% | 72% |
| Market dominance | # of markets where we are #1 or #2 | 16 | 10 |
| Profitability | Net margin, ratio of net profit to total revenue | 12% | 10% |

The team then moves on to reviewing their quarterly priorities, following a similar process to what they used to review the vitals targets. As they review each priority, they discuss the context for how they either achieved it or what caused it to fall short. Again, the key is team learning. As they close the review of the previous quarter's priorities and vitals targets, they turn the corner to begin establishing their priorities for the next quarter.

They use the Objective and Key Result (OKR) framework, popularized in *Measure What Matters* by John Doerr, to first establish their handful of big priority objectives, then determine what success will look like for each by establishing key results. They consider what milestones they want to hit to reach their annual goals, emergent needs that have arisen, and anything they want to do to improve their operating system. While the OKR format is used in this example, teams should feel empowered to use any goal-setting format they feel comfortable with. What matters is that the goals are clear and measurable, not that they follow the OKR framework. There are several goal-setting formats that can help teams drive Focus.

Based on their annual goals, the team decides to prioritize building the marketing engine, beginning with hiring a new marketing manager and sending out proposals for ten conferences, hoping to secure five speaking slots. To meet the annual goal of becoming a best place to work, they decide to start experimenting with a four-day workweek with two pilot teams.

When they consider emergent needs, the Chief Finance Officer flags the upcoming audit, and the team adds getting a clean bill of financial health to their quarterly priorities. Finally, based on their recent Org Health Assessment results, the CEO suggests the team spend time learning about and implementing Agreements as a first step toward addressing their struggles with Cohesion.

The final quarterly priorities look like this:

## Team Quarterly Priorities

| Objective | Key Results | Target | Lead |
|---|---|---|---|
| Build the marketing engine | Hire marketing manager | Manager hired | Lena |
| | 10 conference proposals | 10 | Lena |
| | 5 speaking slots | 5 | Lena |
| Experiment with 4-day workweek | 2 teams experiment with 4-day workweek for 2 months | 2 | Georgie |
| Clean audit | Receive clean bill of financial health | Audit | Quentin |
| Strengthen Cohesion | Complete Agreements training | Training | Marjorie |
| | Adopt 3 Agreements as leadership team | 3 | Marjorie |

With a new set of vitals targets and quarterly priorities to guide their strategic focus, the leadership team is clear on what matters most to accomplish in the coming quarter. They're ready to hit the ground running.

# Flexibility, Learning, and Progress

In March 2020, as cities around the world went into lockdown in response to the COVID-19 pandemic, organizations went into crisis mode. Many companies lost significant business overnight, nonprofits lost funding, and everyone in the service industry scrambled to figure out how to stay open safely.

"We used to plan everything three months out," one leader reflected. "And then COVID happened, and three months seemed like an eternity." After the first few days, I called my team together and we decided to begin setting monthly priorities. We simply 'didn't know what the future would hold, so we needed to shorten our planning window."

Teams that have learned how to drive their Focus efforts while being agile can find Focus in just about any context, even during the first few months of COVID. While many teams had to make significant adjustments to their plans, those that were used to the practice of setting and adjusting priorities knew what to do. They started setting new ones and quickly adjusted as they tried new ideas.

In a crisis situation, Focus can become a lifeline. This does not mean sticking doggedly to the original plan when it no longer makes sense but rather employing the tools of Focus to help weather a particular storm.

Strong Focus is a guide, but these goals are not written in stone. Part of an effective Focus lies in finding the balance between committing to priorities and thoughtfully pivoting in response to changing dynamics. **Strong Focus is also flexible.**

We want to commit to priorities without overcommitting to them. At the end of the day, the process of setting and monitoring goals is what makes the biggest difference, even more than the goals themselves. We hold them as important and we bring attention and intention to them, but we also recognize when a particular goal has outlived its usefulness—even if this deviates from our plan.

**The real outcome of Focus is learning and progress, even more so than hitting a specific target.** The act of setting goals helps teams focus on the right thing, even if they miss the target.

## Rhythm and Focus

Within the 6 Levers, Rhythm and Focus are a power combo. The Rhythm Lever leverages the power of habit to ensure the most essential strategic activities are not left subject to chance. When we're working with teams to improve organizational health for the long haul, this is where we often see the biggest unlock.

**To achieve strong Focus, teams must incorporate regular goal-monitoring into their Rhythms.** If you don't have a meaningful Rhythm to monitor your priorities and targets, Focus will fall off and lose energy. Clear Focus makes Rhythms more meaningful because, within each meeting or Rhythm, the team has a clear objective to focus on. The purpose of the Rhythm becomes to drive those priorities forward.

We'll talk more about how Focus and Rhythm work together in Chapter 6.

# It's Hard, but It's Worth It

Most leaders would agree that goals are important. However, most leaders do not have an effective system for setting and monitoring goals. If you ask the average leader what their team's goals are for the next three to twelve months, you might be surprised by what you hear. That's because, whether we like to admit it or not, effective goal-setting is hard. It's hard to create goals that find a balance between measurability and meaning. It's hard to monitor goals with rigor, consistency, and an appreciation for nuance. And it's hard to decide when to pivot and when to stay the course.

The good news is that it will get easier. Effective goal-setting—or creating Focus with your team—is a practice. As teams get in more reps with it, they will get better. Embracing a tool like the Focus Equation can feel awkward at first, but with practice, it can become second nature.

## Recap of the Focus Lever

The Focus Lever equips teams to navigate the complex nature of collaborative work and elevate priorities, targets, and strategies that matter most. A team with strong Focus has clear priorities, a consistent process to develop those priorities, and a system to monitor them.

**Questions for Reflection**

1. Does your team have a process to collaboratively develop priorities, both in the short term and long term?
2. How consistently does your team monitor your priorities?
3. Are you clear on what the organization-wide priorities are?
4. Out of all 6 Levers, does strengthening Focus seem like one of the priorities for your organization to work on?

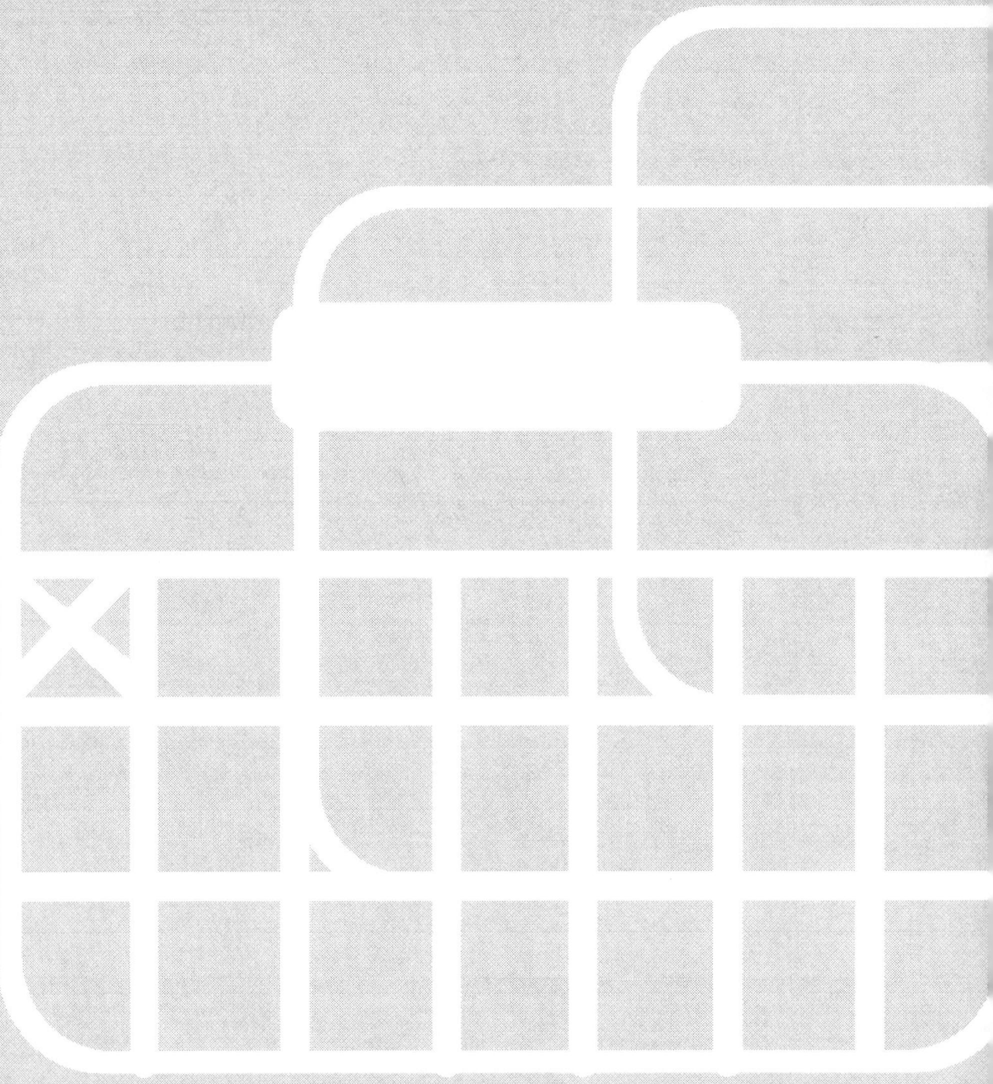

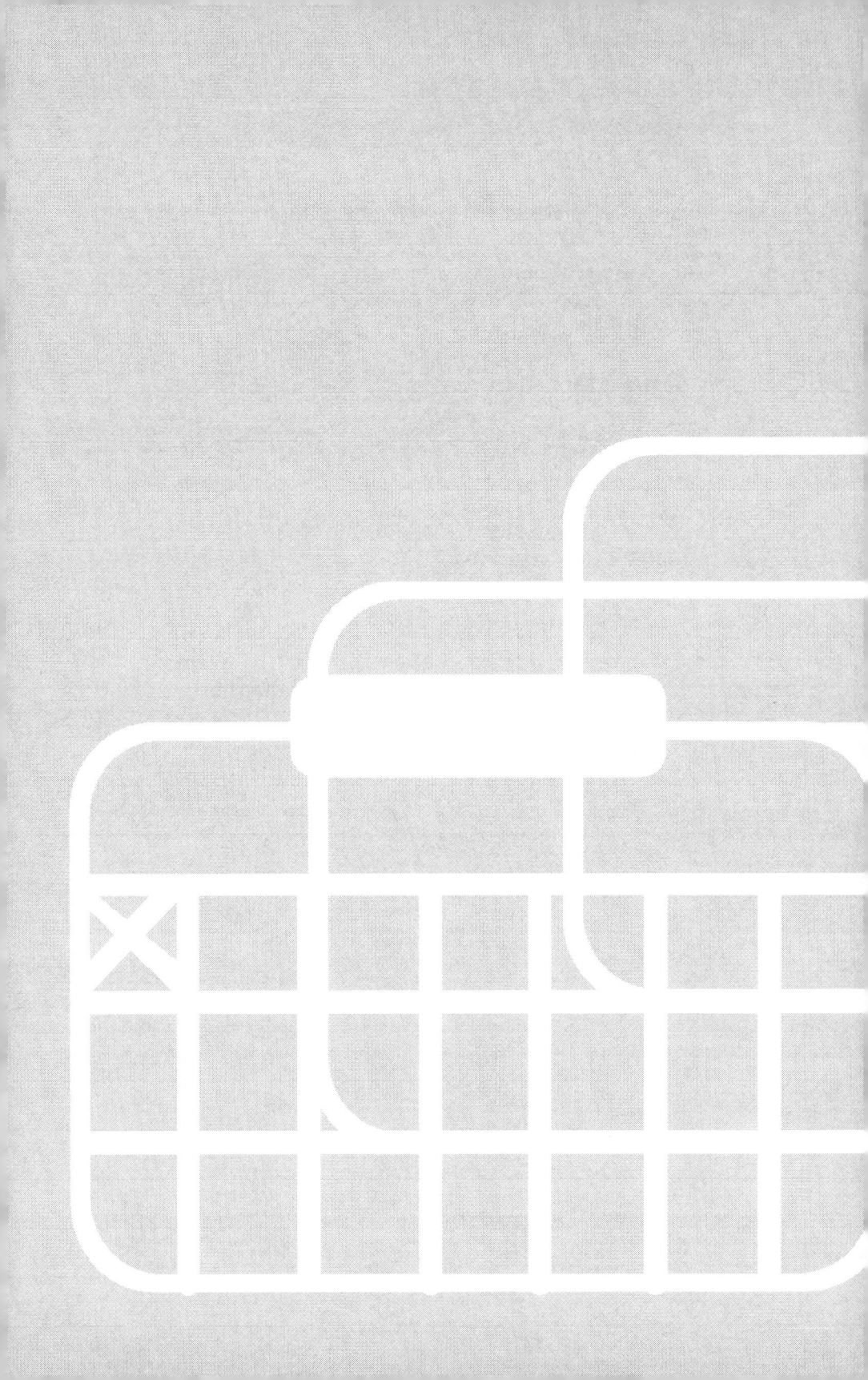

# Rhythm

# Rhythm

How do big ideas come to life? In any organization or team, new ideas sprout constantly. But when it's a big idea—one that will take years, significant investment, and incredible commitment—how does one go from idea to reality?

At World Wide Technology, one such big idea was the creation of the Advanced Technology Center (ATC), a groundbreaking concept of a physical lab to showcase new technologies across several different vendors. Jim Kavanaugh, the CEO of WWT, saw tremendous potential in this big idea, and he convened a weekly two-hour meeting to talk about it—every Friday for years.

In his early career, Josh sat in on these Friday meetings, a junior employee watching from the sidelines as the most senior leaders of this global tech firm discussed the center. Jim would convene the meeting to talk through the opportunities selling into the center and the full solutions the center was producing across several vendors. And every Friday, Jim would remind the group of the vision he saw—what he believed the ATC would do for WWT's business.

The meeting was incredibly powerful for many reasons: the consistency, the commitment, the intellectual rigor, and the results. The meeting was anchored in a clear purpose, and Jim reminded the group of that purpose each time. The team not only committed to this meeting every week, but the agenda of the meeting followed an effective, consistent cadence, as well. This was the first time Josh saw such rigor in sticking to a focused agenda. For the first fifteen or twenty minutes, they would check in on data center opportunities, both for accountability to the sales team and for celebration when they won opportunities. Next, they'd move on to activities happening within the ATC—such as which customers were doing demos and upcoming walkthroughs. Then, they'd talk about what was next for the ATC and other issues in the marketplace that the ATC could address.

Beyond the agenda, the meeting always started on time and ended on time. It was full of healthy debate and resulted in decisions and clear action items.

The results speak for themselves: the advanced technology center—which began with two hundred square feet of space, has now grown to a massive fifty-thousand-square-foot facility. The company itself is now the largest Black-owned business in the United States.

As an athlete his entire life, Josh was well-accustomed to the power of habit in a personal and team context—but this was his first time seeing the power of habit in a professional context. Strong team habits create clarity, keep the team anchored to a bigger vision, and drive a focus on the work that matters. In the case of the Friday meetings, they kept the team of busy leaders focused on a priority that mattered a great deal.

The Rhythm Lever consists of meetings, communications, and processes that serve as organizational habits. **Rhythm leverages the power of habit to ensure the most essential strategic activities are not left subject to chance.**

# How Habits Work: The Power of Habit

If we want to get personally healthy, we know the habits we need to build: exercise, nutrition, therapy, meditation, and drinking lots of water. We understand that one workout or a single therapy session won't suffice. Achieving lasting health requires enduring behavior changes and the cultivation of new habits. The same is true for teams.

At a personal level, we can call upon Charles Duhigg's insights from *The Power of Habit: Why We Do What We Do in Life and Business* to understand this process. We understand that habits involve a cue, routine, and reward. The cue triggers a behavior, the routine is the behavior itself, and the reward is what we gain from it. It's a loop hardwired into our brains, and understanding this loop equips us to make meaningful changes in our personal lives.

Habits wield a profound influence on individuals due to their ability to shape behaviors and outcomes. They can turn into the building blocks of our daily lives, determining whether we inch closer to our goals or drift away from them. The impact of habits is substantial because they are not just actions but rather the driving force behind consistent, intentional actions. Cultivating positive habits unlocks the potential for sustainable success, as they provide the framework for achieving long-term objectives. The transformative power of habits lies in their capacity to make certain actions almost automatic, requiring less conscious effort over time.

Teams are no different. They also operate within this cycle of habit formation. To boost organizational health, teams need to create enduring behavior change and to develop new habits. Just like personal health, organizational health is a function of consistent, intentional actions.

Picture a team that fails to prioritize the most essential strategic activities. They don't have a system in place to follow up with and monitor priorities. Rather than being productive, meetings are tedious, overwhelmed by tactical matters with no clear objective. Calendars are packed, yet it feels like little substantial work is being accomplished. The team makes no significant progress toward its most important goals. Chaos, disorganization, and overwhelm prevail. There's a stark disconnect between daily tasks and the strategic vision, and meetings seem to be the universal solution to every problem. Gossip becomes the norm, as people lack an effective way to address issues directly.

But it doesn't have to be this way. If teams realign their incentives and intentionally design their habits to support their overarching goals, they can harness the tremendous force that habits offer to drive positive change and foster organizational health. The ripple effect of positive habits within a team is often more powerful than at the individual level. While personal habits can certainly enhance one's life, when teams collectively embrace and reinforce beneficial habits, the impact is exponential. A team's collaborative efforts, combined with shared habits, create momentum that propels the team members toward their common objectives with greater effectiveness and a greater sense of purpose and meaning.

## Understanding the Root of Bad Habits

Bad habits often take root due to a combination of factors, one of which is misaligned incentives. Just as individuals are often driven by rewards and punishments, teams and organizations operate under a similar paradigm. When incentives within a team favor short-term gains or suboptimal behaviors, bad habits can thrive.

Consider a scenario where team members are rewarded or recognized for completing tasks quickly rather than for the quality of their work. In such an environment, there's a strong incentive to cut corners, leading to a bad habit of rushing through projects. Similarly, if team performance is measured solely by meeting arbitrary deadlines and not by achieving strategic objectives, the team might fall into the habit of prioritizing the urgent over the important.

When leaders or managers unintentionally incentivize behavior that doesn't align with the organization's Identity and long-term goals, it can foster bad habits across the team. A leader who frequently cancels or reschedules meetings may inadvertently communicate that such commitments are not a priority. Consequently, this habit may spread throughout the team, leading to a lack of accountability and follow-through on important tasks.

## Why Team Habits Matter

Organizational health is the sum of thousands of small actions. Just like a marathon is the sum of little steps, and a finished book is a sum of words and pages, organizational health is the sum of hours, days, and weeks. Organizational health is accomplished in the Rhythm of these micro-actions—one step at a time, one meeting at a time, and one hour at a time. All this takes willpower.

Teams unlock incredible value in routinizing the smaller steps to the bigger goals. The more automatic we can make these routine activities, the less effort it will take to do them.

We talked in Chapter 1 about how every organization has an org OS, but sometimes they aren't intentionally designed. It's similar with team habits. Every team has habits, but the question is whether they're intentional habits that are leading toward organizational health or default habits that are not.

**By thoughtfully designing our team habits, we can move out of this default, accidental way of operating and into an intentional**

**way of working where the system is engineered to achieve our goals.** There's no better way to understand a team's culture and organizational health than by understanding its habits.

## Low Intention, Low Impact

Rashad checked his watch for the fifth time as Valeria called on Natalie to share her updates. The leadership team had already burned through sixty minutes of its seventy-five-minute weekly meeting as the participants provided updates on various projects and teams. The events team update had spiraled into a discussion about possible locations for the fall retreat that was still six months away. The sales update led to several questions from the marketing director. Rashad felt like he was watching a tennis match as the two went back and forth, coordinating details of an upcoming campaign that didn't involve any of the other eight members of the team.

As the program director, Rashad knew skipping the meeting wasn't an option, but he found them agonizing, especially on a day like today when he had an important, urgent issue and needed the team's input to discuss it. Instead, he had to sit through the chaotic jumble of side discussions and undisciplined conversation. Rashad tried to jump in at the beginning of the meeting to flag his issue, but Valeria smiled, brushed him off, and proceeded with her usual format of calling on leaders one by one.

Natalie, the Chief of Staff, spent five minutes reminding everyone about the new procedure for expense reports and budgeting. Rashad had to fight not to roll his eyes. *"Well, that could've been an email,"* he thought to himself.

With five minutes remaining in the meeting, Rashad finally had his chance to speak. "I do have updates about how the water project is going," he said. "But first, we need to talk about the Trees a Million initiative."

The new program was set to launch next month and was facing serious hurdles. One of the three major donors funding the program had decreased their commitment by 60%, and the company providing the seedlings was having trouble sourcing all the trees because of supply chain issues.

"If we don't resolve these problems in the next couple of weeks, we're going to have to pull the plug," Rashad said, two minutes after the meeting was supposed to end.

Valeria noted the time and asked if everyone could stay an extra few minutes to discuss, but everyone except Valeria and Rashad had to get to another meeting. Valeria and Rashad spent ten minutes discussing possible next steps but concluded that they couldn't make any major decisions without marketing, sales, and finance involved.

Rashad left the meeting more frustrated than when it started, wondering, *"What is the point of a meeting if we never talk about what matters most?"* It felt like a missed opportunity to resolve an important issue while all the critical players were present. Rashad felt that the leadership team was failing at its responsibility to make timely decisions for the well-being of the organization. They could have made progress, but instead, less-impactful issues sucked up all the time.

This type of meeting is all too common on teams. Meetings aren't often intentionally designed, and they're not in the Rhythm of concentrating on their areas of greatest Focus. As a result, they lack impact.

# Essential Team Practices

Shaun had just completed his weekly team meeting and was feeling pretty good about himself. The team had gotten through the entire agenda he'd put together in advance and managed to end on time. He'd been running this meeting for a couple of months and felt like he was starting to get the hang of it.

A colleague stopped him in the hall.

"You know, Shaun," she said, "do you realize we managed to get through the entire agenda without talking about any of our most important issues?"

This conversation was a wake-up call. She was right. The team spent all this time in meetings but rarely had space to solve the most important emergent problems they were facing. Everything was predetermined.

This meeting (and so many others) 'wasn't effective for several reasons:

**The team didn't take the time to prioritize its most urgent and important topics to discuss.**

In many meetings, the team talks about everything except what's most important, or the team prioritizes the less important topics. Oftentimes, individuals know what's most important to them, but the team hasn't taken the time to define what's most important to the team as a whole. As a result, everyone fights to give their update or discuss their issue with no understanding of how important it is relative to other issues.

**The team didn't intentionally design the agenda.**

The team hasn't aligned on the overall objective and agenda of the meeting, so there are no clear criteria for whether the meeting is working or not. Meetings are far more impactful when the team takes the time to define the objective and intentionally design the agenda around that objective.

### The team didn't have space for emergent issues.

We work in dynamic, ever-changing organizations, yet we often work off a fixed agenda that doesn't leave space for important, emergent issues. We need meetings that are structured to make space for emergent challenges.

These issues are common in organizations, but there is hope. Let's look at how teams can design effective organizational habits by pulling the Rhythm Lever.

## Building Team Habits

In the Rhythm Lever, teams learn to build strong organizational habits in the form of meetings, communications, processes, and shared experiences. **When we don't create strong Rhythms, we leave the most essential team practices subject to chance.** Often, this looks like a team identifying an activity as important but then forgetting about it because there's no system to monitor that goal or ensure the goal happens.

Team Alpha decides their Cohesion is lacking and they'd like to focus on team relationship-building. Everyone loves the idea, but then six months later, nothing has changed.

Alternatively, Team Beta also decides their Cohesion is lacking and they'd like to focus on team relationship-building. With that strategic activity in mind, they ask, "How can we accomplish this goal?" The team decides to experiment with two new Rhythms: adding a check-in to their weekly meeting to help the team connect and scheduling quarterly team get-togethers to relax and talk.

Team Alpha didn't build a habit around these essential team practices, and as a result, Cohesion didn't happen.

**Rhythms are a powerful way to build habits around essential team practices.**

What are these essential team practices? They are any aspects of the org OS that are important to bring regular focus to. See the graphic for examples.

### Essential Team Practices

- Monitoring goals, letting go of goals that didn't work, and re-prioritizing goals when necessary
- Annual and quarterly strategic planning
- Creating space to resolve urgent issues
- Sharing key updates that fuel collaboration and strengthen communication
- Following up on action items the team committed to
- Reflecting on a past year or quarter and drawing conclusions about what went well and what didn't
- Deepening team connection and trust
- Continuously improving and learning
- Streamlining processes to address issues

These essential team practices may not sound glamorous or exciting, but when they're executed consistently and effectively, they ladder up to the big goal of an intentionally designed org OS. It's similar to a marathon: every step of training is not exciting, but the end result is.

If you're thinking, *"I've tried these things before, and they haven't been impactful,"* we' encourage you to think about these essential team practices in the context of Rhythm design and as part of your overall org OS. It's possible these activities haven't been impactful because they haven't been connected to your intentionally designed organizational operating system. Keep reading to learn how to do this.

# Why You Need Structure to Flow

Imagine a swarm of people dancing at a salsa club. It's incredible to watch as pairs of dancers take the same basic steps—forward, back, forward, back—and creatively apply them in complex, intricate, and creative ways. It's hard to believe it's all built on the same basic structure.

For salsa dancing to work, a dancer needs to know the steps. Otherwise, it's dancing but not salsa. The steps are critical, but they aren't the goal. The goal is the feeling of motion, the joy, the vibration in the air of all these pairs of people moving to the same beat but doing their own thing.

To unlock that joy and all those endorphins, the steps and structure have to come first. In the Rhythm Lever, too, the structure must come first. At first glance, the structure of a meeting may feel overly rigid. It's equivalent to a first salsa dancing class. It's not all that fun as you're counting out beats and fumbling to get your feet in the right place. You have to focus on the structure until it becomes muscle memory. Then, 'the magic happens.

Most people don't want to nerd out about their organizational design or their org OS. They want it to work so they can spend more time on the stuff that matters to them. This is most visible with Rhythms.

**You've got to spend time getting the structure right so you can then forget about it and focus on the stuff that matters most—addressing the most important issues.**

# Designing Your Rhythms

One of the more counterintuitive results of intentional Rhythm design is that it creates more time. When Rhythms are intentionally designed to execute the highest-impact activities, it eliminates the need for many other meetings that pop up in between Rhythms.

## The Perils of the Open Door

Many leaders tell their teams, "My door is always open," with the good intention of being approachable and creating a safe space for dialogue. However, this open-door policy can also signal lazy or nonexistent Rhythm design. Instead of intentionally designing Rhythms to account for the topics that are often discussed in pop-in meetings, leaders allow for a catch-all to handle anything and everything. The open-door policy often turns into a nonstop stream of traffic in and out of a leader's office, putting more strain on an already busy schedule.

The perils of the open-door policy are often a signal that the team needs a new Rhythm or two to create space to address whatever issues are presented during those walk-ins and to process and disseminate the information 'coming in.

Here are a couple of notes before diving into Rhythm design.

### Not everything needs to be a meeting.

When teams see a communication or coordination need, it's common to default to a meeting. It seems like the only idea we can come up with. Then suddenly, we see that our calendars are full. Rhythm design helps teams think intentionally about every new Rhythm they create and think creatively about how to answer their needs. Sometimes, the answer is a new meeting, but oftentimes, it's possible to accomplish the same goals asynchronously or by adding a new segment to an existing Rhythm.

### A single drumbeat is not a rhythm.

Rhythms are recurring. This doesn't mean they need to happen forever, but when we're thinking about Rhythm design, look for habits and patterns, not one-off communications or meetings.

Intentional Rhythm design has several components: the why (purpose), the what (type), and the how (team and timeline).

# The Why: Purpose

A team can consider creating a new Rhythm for many reasons. Here are a few scenarios that might warrant designing and implementing a new Rhythm:

- We want to build team Cohesion by spending more time connecting with each other intentionally.
- We want to bring more Focus to our financial health.
- We are in a moment of crisis and want the ability to make fast, collective decisions.
- We want to celebrate our wins as a team in a more intentional way.
- We want to create a culture of feedback.

- We need greater coordination on one complex project to prevent miscommunication and information gaps.
- We want new employees to understand how we work and our big goals.

Begin by identifying the goal of this new Rhythm. What is the activity to which the team wants to bring more focus and intentionality? Ensure the goal of the Rhythm is clear to everyone participating.

## The What: Type

We have good news: not every Rhythm has to be a meeting. After the team determines the goal of the Rhythm—the why—the next question is, "What's the best format to achieve this goal?" This begins by choosing a Rhythm type.

> **Types of Rhythms**
> - Meetings
> - Processes
> - Communications

Before choosing a Rhythm type, consider the following questions:

- Is the purpose of the Rhythm to share information in one direction without requiring discussion?
- Does the activity require discussion, and if so, is it a simple discussion or a more complex discussion?
- Does the activity require feedback? Could that feedback be effectively gathered asynchronously?
- Is there a tech tool that could help accomplish this goal?

With these answers in mind, let's look at the three types of Rhythms: meetings, processes, and communications.

## Meetings

Consider this example of the Grove International team choosing a meeting format. During the event season, everyone's job changed. As the small team prepared for their annual global conference, everyone became part of the event team, regardless of job description.

As the event director, Madelyn's job was to oversee everything that went into organizing the four-day, five-hundred-person conference: travel logistics, programming, registration, merchandise, and guest speakers. One day, two months before the team would travel to Kampala, Uganda, for the conference, Madelyn had an epiphany while sorting badges and thinking about her to-do list.

"Corinne," she said suddenly. "Those weekly meetings to coordinate everything have worked well for the last two months."

"Yeah," Corinne said, focused on untangling lanyards.

"But this close to the conference, it's not enough. Too much is changing every day."

"Hmm," Corinne said, looking up. "I think you're right. Want to try a daily stand-up?"

The team started the next morning with a fifteen-minute daily meeting Madelyn called Triage. The purpose was for the twenty-person team to flag issues that arose overnight, triage them, and prioritize work for the day. Comments included:

- "One of the hotels had a flood. They think most of the rooms will be fine in time, but we may need to relocate five or six guests."

- "Just an update that we did secure the club for the closing party. It was a tough negotiation, but we landed it."
- "Great news and not-so-great news: the Vice President of Rwanda is confirmed as the keynote speaker. But unfortunately, she's requesting we pay for first-class flights for her and all four of her children."

This quick Triage stand-up allowed the team to coordinate on emergent issues in real time. After the conference, they didn't need it anymore. This stand-up is an example of a meeting Rhythm.

Many times, a team's needs can be met with processes or communications. A new meeting is not always the answer. But we're not advocating for eliminating meetings altogether. Meetings can be an incredibly effective tool for resolving issues and removing blockers. A meeting can be what we traditionally think of as a meeting, but it can also simply be shared time.

Consider a new meeting Rhythm when the target activity is best or solely achieved with shared time, includes information that will likely prompt questions or discussion, needs in-depth discussion among the team, or includes urgent issues that need to be resolved quickly.

Meetings can include stand-ups, one-on-one meetings with a leader and employee, or shared time for the team to connect.

## Processes

This process example is from the Royce and Peters accounting firm. Guadalupe started her new job at the firm with normal first-day jitters. She'd switched jobs a handful of times in her career, but the first day still made her nervous. Jun, the HR manager, met her at the door, gave her a tour, got her a cup of coffee, and set her up with the online onboarding guide.

The guide walked through a checklist for Guadalupe to complete on each of her first five days in the office. It included tasks that were general for any employee (reviewing the organizational chart, reading the employee manual) and tasks specific to her department (processes for tax filings, orientation to the main tax software). The guide also listed meetings to schedule for getting-to-know-you conversations with several employees.

By the end of the first day, Guadalupe was in awe. Normally, the first week was a combination of feeling overwhelmed (information overload) and boredom (not knowing how to do anything when she ended up with free time). Instead, she felt energized, excited, and confident. She'd never seen onboarding that was both comprehensive and allowed for her own independent navigation. Because she could see every task on the checklist, she could plan her own time, checking off items between her meetings.

This is an example of an effective process Rhythm. Documenting and replicating core processes helps teams be more efficient, consistent, and effective. Processes are often completed asynchronously and build health outside of shared time.

We recommend using a process when the key strategic activity you wish to bring more Focus to involves multiple steps that need to be repeated consistently with different people at different times. Examples of processes include content production, product or project creation, and Scorecard updating. Embrace the 80/20 Principle when thinking about processes. The goal is not to document every single process but just the 20% that have 80% of the impact. Focus on the processes with the biggest impact or those that need the most clarity.

A process can occur entirely asynchronously, such as a leader updating their team's Scorecard. Other times, a process requires synchronous time. This could look like an onboarding process that includes several introduction meetings, or Scorecard updating that happens in real time during the weekly Leadership Team Meeting.

## Communications

And finally, an example of communications, the third type of Rhythm, from the customer service team at Wiggle & Co. Every Friday, the team takes time to celebrate. Each of the eight team members posts their win from the week in the shared channel of the team messaging app, including:

- "Got four five-star reviews!"
- "I made a woman cry—the good kind, though. She was so happy I got her a refund and was nice to her."
- "My son won his Taekwondo tournament! Not work related, but I wanted to share anyway."

With each post, the team replies with emojis, encouragement, and joy. Bertie was skeptical at first when Kaitlyn suggested this. The team was discussing ways to build a more positive culture and help everyone feel more connected despite being geographically spread out across four states and two countries.

Bertie normally did not like any kind of team-building or what he called "forced happiness." But to his surprise, he found he looked forward to this simple ritual every Friday. It made everyone smile to end the week celebrating wins.

This is an example of a communication Rhythm that builds a habit around the key strategic activity of team connection. Communications Rhythms are often about sharing key information with the right people at the right time, but they can also be about team connection or asynchronous conversation.

Consider creating a communication Rhythm when the key strategic activity you want to build habits around includes information flowing in one direction, requires time for a recipient to absorb information in order to provide feedback, or needs little to no discussion among the team. Examples of communications are email blasts and reminders or key updates about specific topics, such as finance or HR.

At times, a communication starts out simple enough to manage via email or group chat. However, as questions pop up or dissenting opinions arise, the communication turns into dozens of emails or multi-thread chats that are difficult to follow. Now, it's time to reconsider the medium. If it's getting tense or too complex, it's probably time to switch to a conversation.

## The How: Team and Timeline

Once the team has determined the purpose and type of Rhythm, two questions remain.

### Who needs to be included?

Consider which team members need to be involved or will be affected by this Rhythm. The temptation is often to include everyone in everything, which leads to overwhelm and overflowing inboxes. At other times, leaders don't consider the full breadth of who is affected by a Rhythm. Either extreme can cause problems.

### What is the cadence of the Rhythm?

Consider the logical cadence of a Rhythm, whether it's daily, weekly, monthly, quarterly, or annually. Also, consider whether the Rhythm needs to exist in perpetuity or just for a season. Employee onboarding will likely be relevant forever (albeit in need of updating periodically). However, a daily stand-up that was created to respond to an emergent crisis (a pandemic or staffing shortage, for example) will only need to be in place as long as the crisis lasts. Don't continue Rhythms after they're no longer relevant.

Consider decommissioning a Rhythm if it starts to check any of the following boxes:

- The meeting or activity's goals are met.
- The meeting has become less relevant, or the season that called for the meeting has passed.
- The meeting Rhythm hinders productivity.
- Priorities have changed in such a way that the meeting is no longer necessary in its current format.
- Another channel or format may prove more effective.

# The Three Meetings Every Team Needs

The Operating Cycle is a slate of three meetings that every team needs to be healthy. When teams adopt this meeting structure, they are blown away by the results. These meetings start to make a big difference in how the team operates—both inside and outside the meeting. Each of these meetings is the result of years of research, iteration, and learning. They've been tried and tested with hundreds of organizations, and each is built around an agenda that was intentionally designed to achieve particular activities.

**The Operating Cycle**

1. Weekly Leadership Team Meeting
2. Quarterly Sync
3. Annual Sync

The three meetings are the weekly Leadership Team Meeting, the Quarterly Sync, and the Annual Sync.

## The Weekly Leadership Team Meeting

Get it on the calendar every week for ninety minutes. If you can't swing ninety minutes, go for seventy-five. If you can't do it every week, do it biweekly. The point is to consistently sit down with your leadership team to run through your most important strategic activities.

The Leadership Team Meeting (LTM) includes several essential team practices: to connect with the team, provide important updates, monitor progress on goals, follow up on past action items, and talk about emergent issues. The LTM is one of the most important Rhythms that teams can adopt, and here's why. First, it builds in time to review strategic priorities, ensuring they stay top of mind.

Second, the LTM builds in time for teams to work on their most urgent and important issues every week. This idea breaks from a set agenda where participants are expected to have the agenda completely predetermined. Instead, leaders are encouraged to bring urgent and important topics with the goal of discussing them and finding a way forward by the end of the meeting.

## The Quarterly Sync

Schedule the Quarterly Sync at the end of each quarter so the team can hit the ground running in the new quarter. The Quarterly Sync needs a solid three to four hours, and the time is split between looking back (retrospective) and looking forward (goal-setting).

The purpose of the Quarterly is to connect with the team, reflect on the previous quarter and solidify learning, set goals for the next quarter, and celebrate wins. During the Quarterly Sync, teams reflect on the priorities and vitals targets they set from the previous quarter, focusing on learning and continuous improvement. From that learning, they align on the priorities for the next quarter or semester. Setting priorities in the near term allows teams to break their big annual goals or even three-year goals into more manageable pieces. It also provides fuel as teams see the progress they are making toward their big goals.

## The Annual Sync

The Annual Sync follows much the same structure as the Quarterly Sync. Schedule the Annual for the end of your year (either calendar or fiscal), and allow for an entire day.

The purpose of the Annual is to connect with the team, reflect on the previous year and solidify learning, set goals for the next year, and celebrate wins. It's an essential Rhythm because it helps teams close up the previous year and bring thematic Focus to the next one.

◆ ◆ ◆

To build strong Rhythm within your team and create that feeling of flow, we encourage leaders to embrace the balcony and dance floor metaphor. When you're on the dance floor, you're focused on the details in execution mode. When you go up to the balcony, you can see the full dance floor and how all the pieces are moving together. This metaphor reminds us of the importance of both zooming out to understand how your entire set of Rhythms are working and zooming in to dive into each individual Rhythm and ensure it is working effectively.

# How Rhythm Enables Focus

Have you ever revisited annual goals at the end of the year, only to discover you forgot about half of them?

It's a common scenario that prompts an annual scramble to cram activities into the last couple weeks of the year. This is why Focus needs Rhythm. Strong Rhythms reinforce Focus and keep key priorities top of mind.

When they're well-designed, every Rhythm is rooted in clear objectives. Each meeting of the Operating Cycle puts Focus center stage, pulling up the Scorecard to monitor or review. Once you've clarified your Focus, your team knows the most important priorities. **Rhythms ensure you keep those priorities top of mind for the entire year.** We often find that after reviewing Annual Goals at a Quarterly Sync, we have a renewed sense of Focus. We're reminded of what is most important.

The Rhythm is also an opportunity to intentionally adjust the goals. We often get the question, "How do I know when to stay the course and when to pivot?" The answer is that our goal-setting system must be structured enough to be effective but flexible enough to remain relevant. When the context has changed (whether from external factors or because you've learned something), rigidly sticking to the same goals will not help. When the context changes, we need to revisit and refine our goals.

The effect of this Rhythm and Focus combo starts to take hold after about a month of practice. We start to hear feedback like:

- "Having a routine approach to prioritization has ensured my team is on the same page about our focus."
- "We went from being reactive to being proactive. We can respond

- to urgent situations with intention instead of just putting out fires all the time."
- "We used to say 'yes' to nearly everything, but we don't anymore because we are aligned on what it would cost us."

Many leaders feel like they don't have enough time. When they start implementing Focus and Rhythm together, they begin to feel the difference. They can focus on what matters most, say "no" to the rest, and empower their teams to take ownership of different priorities. This is where they start to find more time.

## Progress Over Perfection

Implementing new Rhythms can be awkward and messy at first. This is normal. When a leader is fumbling through a new agenda and trying to manage a tech tool at the same time, they must remember that once they learn the steps, it will get easier.

With Rhythms, we learn by doing—as long as we bring intention to our design. Choose one meeting, and start with building a set of objectives. Define an agenda, then put structure and detail into how you'll facilitate and what tools you'll use. Test, learn,7 and keep trying new things.

In the community of people in recovery from drug or alcohol addiction, there's a saying: "Relapse is part of recovery." The idea is to understand that progress is the goal, not perfection. As humans, we often get caught up in the idea that projects or ideas need to be perfect to be worthwhile or acceptable. That pursuit of perfection can become an enemy of progress.

Remember this as you work to implement changes to your team's Rhythms. Not everything will go smoothly, and that's okay. It's all part of the process. Not all of your efforts will go as well as you'd like, or they might fail completely. This is okay, too. You can always restart and keep going.

When a part of a Rhythm doesn't feel effective, go back to the why. Ask yourself and your team, "Does this new Rhythm or part of the meeting achieve our objective?" If it's not working, change it and try a different tactic. The approach to organizational health is not a one-size-fits-all program, and this holds true for designing Rhythms. Bring a lens of continuous improvement and learning, and adjust as needed. Remember to consider all Rhythms within the context of the heart of work: people and systems.

### Recap of the Rhythm Lever

The Rhythm Lever leverages the power of habit to ensure the most essential strategic activities are not left subject to chance. A team with strong Rhythm has focused and purposeful meetings, can leverage the power of asynchronous Rhythms, and has the tools to iterate on and design their own Rhythms.

**Questions for Reflection**

1. How strong do you think your team's Rhythms are?
2. What one step could you take to strengthen your Rhythm?
3. Out of all 6 Levers, does strengthening Rhythm seem like one of the priorities for your organization?

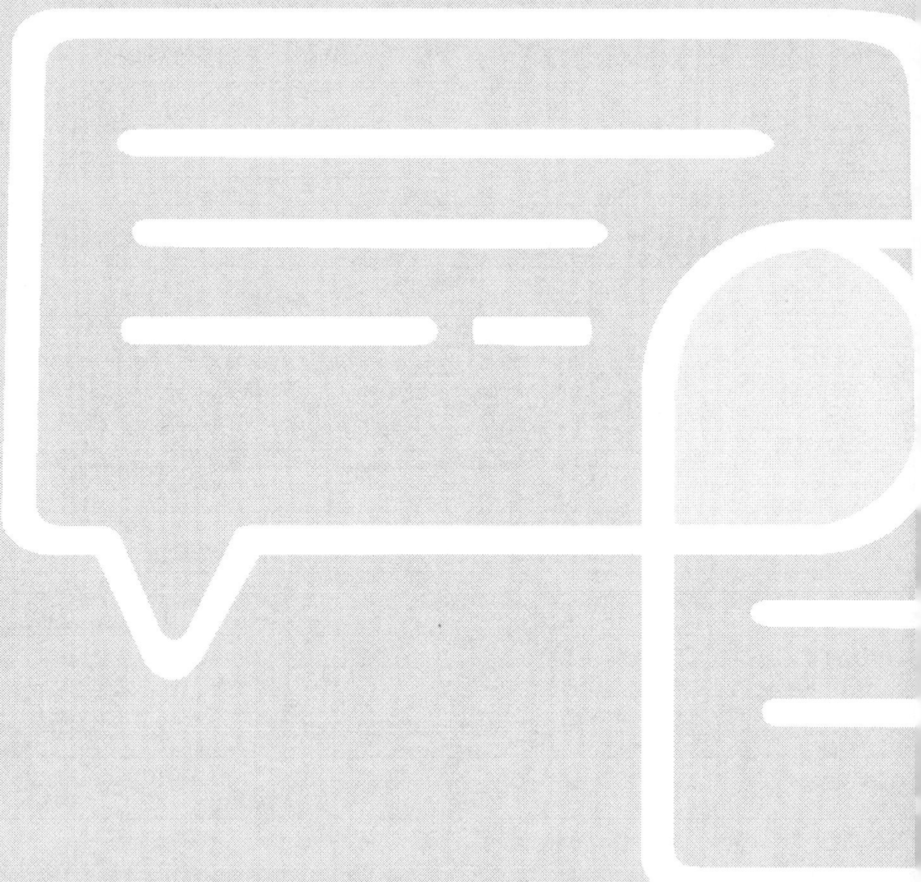

# Cohesion

# Cohesion

Lebron James is one of the best basketball players in the history of the sport. At the 2014 NBA Finals, in his Game 5 postgame interview after his team's loss to the San Antonio Spurs, James was asked by a reporter if he agreed with his teammate Chris Bosh's assessment of the Spurs as the best basketball team he'd ever played against. Lebron's response was immediate and clear. "I would agree. They were the much better team, and that's how team basketball should be played." The 2014 San Antonio Spurs are a testament to the power of team cohesion. The team's style of play during their 2014 championship run has become known as "The Beautiful Game," and while they may not be considered the greatest team of all time, many basketball historians say that their play in the 2014 Finals may be the highest level of basketball ever played.

So, how did they do it? How did a team with no superstars (Tim Duncan was way past his prime, and Kawhi Leonard wasn't in his yet) rise to a level of play never seen before? It boils down to their superior level of cohesion. We define Cohesion as the degree of unity, meaning, and psychological safety shared among a group of people or a team. Cohesion is evidenced by the strength of the relationships that hold individuals together toward a common goal, fostering collaboration, communication, and mutual support.

For the Spurs, it began with a clear and meaningful purpose defined most notably by their team-first mentality and deliberate style of play, a system that was constructed to leverage the wide range of strengths across their roster. But key to their identity was not only the clarity about the type of team they aspired to be but also their unwavering belief in it. Experts described the culture that the Spurs formed around their identity as the pinnacle example of team basketball. While the NBA was moving to super teams that required incredible production from two to three key players, the Spurs went the other way. They had at least eight key contributors in their Finals run, making it possible for one player to have an off night while the team as a whole still thrived. From seasoned veterans to rising stars, each player embraced their role with commitment and reliability.

Complementing their strong identity was a culture of trust that reigned supreme in the locker room. Players felt emboldened to take risks and be creative on the court, knowing they had the unwavering support of their teammates. This mutual respect fostered an environment where psychological safety flourished within the framework of their team-first approach. And this didn't happen by accident. The team was committed to connecting with each other off the court. It was again a part of their identity.

To help build team trust and connection, Coach Pop often took the entire team out to dinner. In fact, this ritual was so important to them that they even went out to eat as a team after the gut-wrenching loss in the 2013 Finals. One player reflected on this team ritual by saying, "I was friends with every single teammate I ever had in my [time] with the Spurs. That might sound far-fetched, but it's true. And those team meals were one of the biggest reasons why. To take the time to slow down and truly dine with someone in this day and age—I'm talking a two- or three-hour dinner—you naturally connect on a different level than just on the court or in the locker room." This commitment to building a cohesive team was clear and deliberate, and it made it possible to know each other and work through conflict. They understood and believed in each other as people. This commitment was clear and deliberate. And because they understood and believed in each other as people, they found working through conflict and tension simply a part of who they were.

The 2014 San Antonio Spurs are a model of teamwork and what can happen when teams take the time to intentionally become more cohesive. Their championship journey exemplified the power of cohesion, showcasing their unity, shared purpose, and a healthy culture of psychological safety and support. They reaffirmed the timeless wisdom often attributed to Aristotle: The whole is greater than the sum of its parts.

# Project Aristotle

One key learning from the 2014 Spurs success is that they did it without superstars. We often think it takes superstars on teams, not just in sports, to realize our wildest dreams. Google had this same wondering as they sought to discover what makes an effective team. Was superstar performance the key ingredient in successful teams, or was it something else? Google's curiosity came from noticing inconsistencies in team performance despite similar skill sets, expertise, and experience. Some teams excelled while others struggled—and Google didn't know why.

A team is simply a grouping of humans, and humans are unpredictable. We're driven by a variety of factors, many of which are invisible to outsiders. We like some things and dislike others. We react with anger to something today that a week later doesn't bother us at all. Human behavior is mysterious. So, what happens when we group humans together in teams? Team behavior also feels like a mystery—and this is the problem Google set out to solve.

Google believed teams were so critical to success that the company launched Project Aristotle in 2012 to help them crack the code. The Google People Operations Team set out to collect data from more than 180 Google teams across different departments and locations. They looked at everything from personality traits to skills, from social interactions to team make-up, and even to individual backgrounds.

Conventional wisdom suggests that a strong team is built with individual superstars. This is not what Google found. What makes a team effective is less about the individuals and more about how the team works together.

Project Aristotle unearthed five aspects of effective teams, as shown in the graphic.

### Five Aspects of Effective Teams

1. **Psychological safety:** Team members feel safe to take risks and make mistakes.
2. **Dependability:** Team members do what they say they will do.
3. **Structure and clarity:** Roles, goals, and decision-making processes are clear.
4. **Meaning:** Team members find purpose in their work.
5. **Impact:** Team members feel that their work is making a difference.

Project Aristotle's findings challenge the conventional wisdom that assembling a team of individual superstars is the key to success. Instead, Google discovered that what truly makes a team effective is how well its members work together. This research identified five critical aspects of effective teams: psychological safety, dependability, structure and clarity, meaning, and impact. When every member embodies these five aspects, the team can collectively reach heights that no lone superstar could attain.

# Understanding the Impact of Teams

Teams are not just the gears in the machinery—they are the engines of success, the bedrock of learning and innovation, and the heartbeat of employee engagement. Teams play a crucial role in shaping an organization's culture, strategy, and impact.

By understanding and empowering their teams, leaders unlock sustainable success and growth. Organizational transformation happens at the team level. Teams are the engine of success across four major workplace dimensions.

## 1. Teams Are the Heartbeat of Employee Engagement

An individual's immediate team shapes their work experience more than any other factor. While the broader organization impacts our work, it's the camaraderie, shared objectives, and daily interactions of our immediate teams that shape and color each employee's overall experience and well-being.

In the early 1900s, Frederick Taylor revolutionized factory work by breaking down every task into its component parts and training every employee to do each task exactly to specification. Eliminate thinking; just execute. In a factory, inconsistency equals lost time and lost money. There's no room for individual expression or opinion.

Organizations of today are not factories, and the means of production are not machines but people. Organizations are dynamic, both because they operate in rapidly changing environments and also because they are fueled by living, breathing humans with a variety of needs, opinions, and ideas. We believe that fundamental human needs should be at the heart of organizational design. And because organizations are driven by people working together, the relationship among those people becomes critically important.

More than the organization as a whole, one's immediate team has an incredible impact on individual employees. The average human will spend one-third of their life at work, and for many, they spend most of their working life as part of a team. Regardless of the greatness of an organization, if an employee has a bad experience on a team, it taints their entire experience of that organization.

In an orchestra, imagine a flute player who likes the director and the brass players but hates the other woodwinds. Even if she loves the music, the mission, the audience, and the concert hall—if she doesn't like her team, it will have a huge impact on her experience of the orchestra as a whole.

## 2. Teams Are the Bedrock of Learning and Innovation

In geology, bedrock is the solid rock—or foundation—beneath looser soil or subsoil. In an organization, teams are the bedrock upon which success is built because they are central to an organization's ability to innovate and collaborate.

This ability comes from the team's proximity to the front lines of the external work of an organization. Teams are the closest to the problems and to the clients' results. Learning happens most frequently and impactfully at the team level. When teams are empowered and designed to leverage learning for growth, this learning translates to innovation.

Modern problems require multidimensional solutions. Teams naturally embody a mix of experiences, expertise, and viewpoints. When functioning optimally, teams become the crucibles where diverse thoughts meld to produce innovative solutions. In an age where innovation is the key differentiator, healthy teams are not just important—they are indispensable.

Building a resilient organization requires a diverse ecosystem. Diversity in thought, approach, and background is an asset in problem-solving and organizational health. A well-functioning organization leverages the diverse skills, experiences, and perspectives of its people and teams, leading to more innovative solutions. This diversity is a critical piece of what makes teams indispensable.

**When we get intentional about empowering and harnessing team learning, we unlock new opportunities to innovate.**

# 3. Teams Bring Strategy to Life

Strategy is the broad strokes of how an organization will accomplish its vision. Without effective execution, strategy is just a dream. Teams are the catalysts that bring each piece of strategy to life, transforming vision into tangible actions. This is why leaders often invest a lot of time and resources to include team-level input in strategic planning efforts. Since teams will be the primary drivers of execution, it's critical that they have buy-in on the larger vision (as well as the necessary resources and tools).

To fulfill this critical role, teams need to be able to set goals, choose strategies, execute effectively, and adapt as needed. Far too often, only a few teams in an organization adopt a process like this, but every team needs these capabilities to ensure sustainable and successful strategy implementation.

Teams aren't only responsible for executing; they also play a pivotal role in shaping strategy. Because teams are the bedrock of learning and innovation, they can provide valuable insight to inform strategy, and this stems from their on-the-ground experiences. This bi-directional relationship allows organizations to respond to evolving challenges and opportunities more effectively. The collective effort of teams throughout the organization both executes and shapes strategy, making it a dynamic and responsive process.

## 4. Teams Shape Culture

Teams are the linchpin for both producing tangible results and shaping organizational culture. Healthy teams are the foundation upon which a company builds a thriving organizational culture.

How is culture formed? Is it from the top down (from the executive level on down)? Or is it from the bottom up?

We believe it's the latter. Leadership teams have more influence than any other team, but the collective influence of all the other teams outweighs the influence of the single leadership team. Teams are the driving force shaping the overall culture. Genuine adoption and cultural molding take place at the team level. Teams are where the beliefs, values, and tenets that define the organization's culture are translated into meaningful rituals. They set the tone for collaboration, communication, and decision-making. When teams embrace and embody the desired cultural attributes, they serve as cultural ambassadors, and their actions become examples for others to follow.

Healthy, high-performing, cohesive teams do more than just honor existing culture—they bring their own microcultures to life. These microcultures strengthen the overall culture and often have a more significant impact on people's level of job satisfaction. A strong team microculture leads to higher engagement and reduced burnout. As teams shape their microcultures through collective beliefs, rituals, and behaviors, they serve as the architects of the organization's culture.

◆ ◆ ◆

Teams, when cohesive, become the engines of an organization's results, resilience, and culture. When leaders foster team autonomy and intentionality, they unlock new opportunities for organizational learning and growth. When teams thrive, they ignite a chain reaction, enhancing the organization's ability to navigate change, foster innovation, and nurture an adaptable culture. When leaders recognize the pivotal role that teams play, they can better steer their organizations toward enduring organizational health.

# Creating the Conditions for Cohesion

Baobab trees are among the strongest and tallest trees on earth. Their bark is fire-resistant, and they can reach nearly one hundred feet in height and thirty feet in diameter as they withstand thousands of years of life in semi-desert conditions.

These incredible, funky trees are resilient, but they aren't indestructible. Wet soil and frost can kill a baobab. Even the strongest trees in the world cannot thrive without the right conditions.

**The Cohesion Lever gives teams practical tools and structures that create the conditions for individuals and teams to thrive.** A team that's high in Cohesion shares a collective sense of purpose, collaborates to define goals and resolve tension, and supports one another, creating an environment where a group of individuals can come together to achieve an objective bigger than the individuals could do on their own. When Cohesion is high, teams can navigate change and drive progress because they have the right conditions for people and teams to thrive. When teams start to strengthen other aspects of their operating system, this builds Cohesion as well.

For teams that are low in Cohesion, every other aspect of the 6 Levers will be an uphill battle. Low Cohesion—more than any other Lever—has a unique power to derail progress and create distractions. If teams are central to organizational health, then they're also central to organizational frustration.

How can a leader actively create the conditions for their team to thrive? We've identified a few core areas.

## Build Psychological Safety

As Project Aristotle showed, psychological safety is essential for a strong team. Patrick Lencioni called out a similar dynamic in his book *The Five Dysfunctions of a Team*. Of his five dysfunctions, the biggest barrier to effective teams is an absence of trust. When we ask groups of leaders what makes their teams effective, our informal research reflects the same findings: the most important component is trust, along with connection and psychological safety.

Amy Edmondson coined the term "psychological safety" and defines it as "a belief that one will not be punished or humiliated for speaking up with ideas, questions, concerns, or mistakes and that the team is safe for interpersonal risk-taking." Team members must be able to trust one another. To build trust, start with human connection.

Psychological safety is not a condition that a leader can engineer easily, but leaders can leverage tools that allow psychological safety to grow over time. Through rituals and shared experiences, team members get to know each other on a deeper level and connect and build trust. We share more about these practical tools later in this chapter.

## Collaboratively Design How Work Works

Effective teams have "a way we do things." There's a shared understanding of how work works, and as a result, the team can spend most of its time working on high-leverage, meaningful activities. Creating this shared understanding doesn't happen by accident. It's created when a leader and a team intentionally design work with the needs of the team top of mind and with team members included in the process. Remember the *with and for* principle from Chapter 1.

**We believe that when people are involved in defining how work works, individuals are more engaged and organizations are more resilient.** Everyone wants to feel like the system is not done "to us" but "with us."

Intentionally designing work leads to clarity—in goals, roles, agreements, norms, mindsets, and how work gets done—and it has transparent structures to facilitate collaboration and communication. This clarity and structure go beyond the organizational chart or design to the organizational operating system. Clarity and structure enable strategy, creativity, and progress. This clarity also helps provide a common language to use when troubleshooting issues or working to continuously improve the operating system.

## Elevate Meaning and Purpose

On a cohesive team, the members are highly engaged in their work. A key driver of this engagement is that the work feels meaningful. Each team member can connect their work to their own personal purpose. They have autonomy in how they complete their work. They feel a sense of belonging.

An intentionally designed org OS can help connect team members to meaning and purpose, which leads to Cohesion. When everyone has a clear understanding of how work works, it helps them understand the meaning behind their work and connect to a wider purpose. Rituals and shared experiences also help connect team members to meaning and purpose, and they especially help individuals feel that they are part of a mission larger than themselves.

Teams that have the highest connection to meaning can see it on two levels: the organizational level and the team level. All too often, teams don't take the time to align on their core purpose and how it connects to the overall identity of the organization. When teams do, it further deepens a sense of meaning.

Clearly defined organizational identity also contributes to a team's ability to find meaning in its work. We encourage teams to go a step further by translating this organization-level identity to their individual teams, creating their own purpose statement and vitals, and going even further to help them see the meaning and impact of their work.

# The Pixar Braintrust

Pixar Animation Studios has produced blockbuster after blockbuster, from *The Incredibles* to *Finding Nemo* to *Cars* and the *Toy Story* franchise. But these iconic films don't start out as winners. According to Ed

Catmull, one of the founders of Pixar, "Early on, all of our movies suck." How does a movie evolve from terrible to blockbuster? The answer lies in a practice called the Braintrust.

Originally, this team of creative minds at Pixar—directors, writers, heads of story—started getting together every few months to review a movie that was in the works. The entire purpose of bringing this team together was to find problems with the storytelling and to find solutions to those problems.

When an author is knee-deep in a book or a painter is nearly done with a painting, it can be difficult to distance oneself enough from the project to view it objectively. But this objective, critical eye is often necessary to help push the project from mediocrity to excellence.

Pixar understands that people deeply involved in bringing a creative dream to life need some objective outside counsel. This is why they intentionally designed it into their org OS. This counsel comes in the form of feedback from people they trust—other creatives who have been in the trenches of similar work and can bring an expert's eye. Pixar also understands that criticism can be challenging. For the Braintrust to work, the team needs to have a high degree of psychological safety.

Each director needs to believe and feel that their team members have their best interests at heart and that they're voicing suggestions for one reason: to make the project the best it can be. It's a safe space.

The Braintrust leverages multiple aspects of a strong team: the power of collaboration, experimentation and iteration (or Momentum, as we call it), and the conditions to thrive. How?

- They built a foundation of strong psychological safety with a high level of trust and nonjudgment. Receiving critical feedback on a creative project requires mutual trust.
- They intentionally designed how work would work through clear

structures and expectations in the meeting. Everyone understood why they were there, what was expected of them, and how they would use the time.
- They elevated meaning and purpose by staying focused on the big objective that every creative is striving for: telling a great story.

The Braintrust has become an integral part of the Pixar creative process and has helped create the conditions for individuals and teams to thrive in a cohesive environment. The result is clearly visible in the long list of hits.

# The Power of Common Language

One great benefit of the 6 Levers is that it provides a common language for teams. When a team has adopted the system, they learn a language that puts into words concepts that felt too abstract before. Instead of being silently frustrated about a meeting that went long, a team member can now say, "I'm feeling a tension around our meeting length. Can we discuss and potentially adopt an Agreement about ending on time?" The rest of the team would immediately understand what she meant by "tension" and "Agreement" and also would know the process to follow based on those keywords.

In *The Speed of Trust: The One Thing That Changes Everything*, Stephen M.R. Covey talks about the central role of trust in all types of relationships. He argues that when trust is high within a team or organization, things can be accomplished more quickly and efficiently. This concept is referred to as "moving at the speed of trust."

How do we build trust? Shared language is one answer. When teams can develop and leverage a common language, they can communicate more effectively and understand each other more readily and rapidly.

This shared understanding reduces misunderstandings, confusion, and potential conflicts that can arise due to miscommunication. Adopting shared language can go a long way in equipping teams to move at the speed of trust. Here are a few other positive impacts of adopting a common language across teams.

## Organizational Culture and Identity

Shared language helps develop strong organizational culture, and it can bring organizational Identity into the day-to-day work of each team. Common language is a powerful tool for shaping norms and behaviors across teams. When employees share a language, it creates a sense of belonging and fosters a cohesive work environment. It enhances team spirit, promotes connectedness, and strengthens the overall organizational culture.

## Knowledge Sharing and Learning

Shared language enables effective knowledge sharing and learning. When employees use a common language, it becomes easier to document and transfer knowledge, best practices, and lessons learned. New employees can quickly integrate into the organization and benefit from existing knowledge, accelerating their learning curve.

# Cohesion in Action

> **Three Practices to Build Cohesion**
>
> 1. Agreements
> 2. Rituals
> 3. Shared Experiences

Project Aristotle went a long way in demystifying what it takes to make a strong team. The logical question that follows is, "How can I do that for my team?" We've identified a handful of practices that help teams begin the process of building Cohesion.

The three practices are Agreements, Rituals, and Shared Experiences.

## Agreements

Individual humans come from unique backgrounds with varied experiences. We are not all starting from the same place, and we all bring our own assumptions into the workplace. We operate as we see fit, behaving in a way that seems logical to us. But our coworkers—who are also operating in a way that seems logical to them—have their own assumptions. Sometimes, these assumptions match. Many times, they don't.

These differences in assumptions, experiences, and expectations often lead to conflict on teams. A common example is around working hours and communication. Team members may have different preferences about when they work. Some prefer to wake up early, and others prefer to start later and work later. In remote, flexible workplaces, some employees may choose to work a couple of hours early in the morning, while others choose to answer emails at 9 p.m. after the kids go to bed.

Different schedules means that emails or messages are flying around at all hours of the day. This isn't necessarily a problem, but it becomes an issue when there are different expectations about those communications.

For example, Penelope, the leader of a ten-person team, has trouble getting to sleep at night, so she regularly cleans out her inbox at 10 p.m. as a way to wind down. The emails aren't urgent, and she doesn't expect her team to respond. At Brent's last job, any time he received an email from his boss, the boss expected a response within thirty minutes, regardless of the time of day. Whenever Brent receives an email from Penelope, he feels obligated to immediately respond because he assumes Penelope expects a response. Meanwhile, Georgette doesn't even see the emails until 8 a.m. because she has turned off her notifications and is sleeping soundly by the time they arrive.

The team has a series of expectations and assumptions that are all hidden. No one has stated these out loud. When expectations and assumptions remain silent, the soil is primed for conflict to grow.

Agreements are a tool to clarify the way work works. They make explicit the team's assumptions about ways of working to resolve and—ideally—prevent conflict. Here's how it could work for Penelope's team.

## 1st: Notice the Tension

Brent realizes he's feeling tension because he doesn't want to answer emails at 10 p.m. but feels obligated to do so whenever anyone sends an email. Brent raises this tension with the team during their weekly meeting. He says, "I've noticed a tension I'm feeling: whenever any of you sends a late-night email, I feel like I have to answer, and it stresses me out."

## 2nd: Validate Whether It's a Team Issue

Penelope asks the team, "Do others feel this same tension?" Georgette says "no" because she ignores emails after 6 p.m., but the others say "yes." The core question is whether this is an issue for a single person or for the entire team.

## 3rd: Identify the Core Issue

The team discusses the issue. Penelope shares about her sleep issues and says that she doesn't expect anyone to reply. Other team members share their variety of responses: some ignore emails, others read but don't reply, and some feel they must reply. The team realizes that the core issue is that they haven't defined expectations around working hours and communications after hours.

## 4th: Propose a Solution

Georgette proposes an Agreement that any message drafted after 5 p.m. be scheduled to be sent first thing the next morning unless it's urgent. The team agrees.

## 5th: Team Collaboratively Decides How to Proceed

The team creates an Agreement to experiment with this possible solution for two months and then revisit it.

We've found that by giving teams a framework and common language to recognize and address tensions, they can more effectively create common ways of working while productively managing—or even preventing—conflict. As teams get better at recognizing tensions, they will begin to address them earlier, leading to a more peaceful environment where conflict doesn't fester and grow.

# Rituals

A great example of a workplace ritual comes from actress Amy Poehler, who started a ritual on the set of *Parks and Recreation*.

When the cast and crew gathered for a wrap-up dinner, she would stand up and toast a team member, then that person would toast another person. This went around the room until everyone had been toasted. Mike Schur, co-creator of *Parks and Recreation*, shared the story, saying, "She'd pick out a second AD or a makeup person or a camera operator. It was just the most wonderful way to end a work experience." Schur valued the experience so much that he continued this tradition on the set of his sitcom *The Good Place*.

Rituals are repeated practices and activities that foster a culture of human connection and belonging. This is a second tool leaders can use to strengthen team Cohesion. The idea is simple: choose an activity that focuses on bringing the team together, and do that activity at a regular cadence (weekly, monthly, annually). The focus of Rituals is building culture, not operations, including:

- Bringing Identity alive
- Celebrating a win
- Connecting
- Shouting out a team member
- Expressing gratitude
- Showing belonging

Here's another example. The product launch team at Beta Corp. organizes a new launch twice a year. The two months prior to the launch is always a high-stress, intense period for the entire team. The leader, Cassie, started a Ritual several years ago that the team affectionately calls "Product Eulogy." The team gets together for a happy hour, and they share stories about everything that went wrong during the launch. At the end of the happy hour, a team member wraps up the session by giving a eulogy to the product. It's a cathartic experience for the team to laugh, complain, and blow off steam. By the end of the eulogy, the team is ready to put this launch to rest and move on to the next.

## Shared Experiences

At Mission Matters Group, the company that incubated 6 Levers, we had been planning for a while to celebrate our tenth anniversary as a company. We postponed it due to COVID-19, and finally in the fall of 2022, we made it happen.

Our ten-person team was spread across four states and two countries, and we convened everyone for a four-day retreat in Arizona. Our goal was partially operational—doing our normal annual retrospective and goal-setting—but also about having fun together. We didn't over-plan it; we trusted that given shared physical space and enough time, our team would take advantage of the opportunity to connect, get to know each other better, bond, and hold meaningful conversations.

A year later, our team was still talking about this retreat as a highlight of their work experience.

This was an example of what we call a Shared Experience, an intentional activity or experience that fosters connection, collaboration, and a sense of belonging on a team. Shared Experiences enhance relationships and deepen understanding among team members. Our most memorable and impactful experiences are most often those we share with others, and by intentionally creating Shared Experiences for our team, we help create the conditions for these meaningful connections to occur.

Shared Experiences could be formal and big, like a team retreat in

Arizona, but they can also be small, short, and informal. A team that chats about their lives in the kitchen as they wait for the morning coffee to brew is having a Shared Experience. Shared Experiences could be team-building or social events, Rituals, collaborative work protocols, or any activity that fosters team learning, growth, and connection.

# Establishing Common Ways of Working Across Teams

Cohesion has two dimensions: within a team and across teams. So far in this chapter, we have focused on Cohesion within a team. It's also important for organizations to consider how Cohesion between teams impacts the overall culture. When more and more teams in an organization adopt common ways of working using the 6 Levers, it will offer powerful benefits and build a culture that feels Cohesive across teams.

Establishing common ways of working across teams will also guard against an organization being a collection of distinct subcultures. You might hear statements like, "Well, on my team, we …" or "That type of stuff doesn't happen on my team." It's good for teams to embrace unique aspects of the way they work, but if it feels like one team is speaking a completely different language from the others, then it will be a challenge to align and collaborate across the organization.

Consider an orchestra and how the different sections work together. The combined efforts of all the sections achieve a sound that is greater than the sum of its parts. The interplay of different instruments and textures creates a rich tapestry of sound, capturing the beauty, essence, and emotion of the music. This also demonstrates what's possible when organizations achieve Cohesion across teams. Establishing common ways of working will benefit organizations across all their teams for three key reasons.

## Agility and Flexibility

When teams adopt common ways of working, it becomes easier to scale operations and adjust. New team members can quickly understand and adapt to established processes, reducing onboarding time. If they need to make changes, they can implement them more efficiently since teams are familiar with the underlying tenets and can collaborate effectively.

An orchestra can make quick changes and adjustments because everyone is running on the same OS. They've agreed to a common way of working, and everyone understands the process, the structure, and how decisions are made.

## Scaling Organization-Wide Focus

Adopting common ways of working and running on 6 Levers promotes alignment with the top-line objectives and strategies of the organization. All too often, a leadership team will set goals for the year that never trickle down to the teams that are responsible for delivering on those goals. When all teams across an organization are running on the same OS, it's much easier to align their goals and Identity to those of the organization as a whole. This is where an organization's goals expand beyond the executive team and spread to the entire organization, with every team rowing in the same direction toward the same big goals.

For the orchestra, every section has the same shared objective—the piece of music they're working on—and they understand their role in achieving that goal and can translate it to individual musicians' efforts.

## Enabling Collaboration

Imagine an orchestra where one section isn't fulfilling its role. Imagine the triumphant moment in a soundtrack without the horn section.

Imagine the lack of dynamism that might occur without a soloist in the woodwinds. Imagine how they would struggle to stay in sync without the percussion section.

However, the impact is even greater than just missing a key section within a performance. Each section plays off each other. When one section is strong, it strengthens another. When one section is slightly off, the other sections adapt responsively. They feed off each other, and they support each other.

The orchestra sections interact with each other. They exchange melodies and harmonies, creating intricate musical conversations and interplay. They support and complement each other, highlighting the unique qualities of each section while blending together harmoniously—creating a result that is greater than the sum of its parts.

Effective collaboration is critical for an orchestra to reach its full potential. **The tools of Cohesion create the conditions for trust and collaboration both within a team and also across teams and departments, enabling cross-team collaboration rooted in efficiency and trust.**

◆ ◆ ◆

Just as the Spurs intentionally created the right conditions to flourish, any team can thrive when they intentionally cultivate the conditions for Cohesion. The Cohesion Lever offers practical tools and structures that create a sense of purpose, collaboration, and support within teams, enabling individuals to unite toward a common goal. High Cohesion equips teams to navigate change and drive progress effectively. Conversely, low Cohesion poses a significant barrier to progress, hindering efforts across many aspects of organizational health. By nurturing psychological safety, trust, clarity, and a sense of belonging, leaders empower teams to unlock their full potential both in teams and across teams.

> ### Recap of the Cohesion Lever
>
> The Cohesion Lever harnesses the power of intentional, unified, and connected teams. A team with strong Cohesion has clear ways of working, an understanding of the importance of psychological safety and how to build it, and the tools to resolve conflict productively.
>
> **Questions for Reflection**
>
> 1. Does your team have clear ways of working that are collaboratively designed?
> 2. Do you feel a strong sense of psychological safety on your team?
> 3. What tools does your team use to resolve conflict?
> 4. Out of all 6 Levers, does strengthening Cohesion seem like one of the priorities for your organization?

# Momentum

# Momentum

Imagine a room filled with eager participants, each armed with spaghetti sticks, tape, string, and a marshmallow. Their challenge? To construct the tallest freestanding structure possible using these elementary materials. It is an experiment designed to uncover the nuances of innovation, collaboration, and the driving force of momentum. This is the Marshmallow Design Challenge.

This peculiar test of creative engineering wasn't the brainchild of a traditional scientist but of a design expert named Peter Skillman. Skillman was on a quest to demystify the dynamics behind teamwork, discovering what fuels innovation in a group setting. The participants: a diverse mix of engineers, architects, business leaders, and an unexpected addition—kindergartners.

As Skillman set the stage, he didn't favor the adults with decades of experience, nor did he handicap the kindergartners due to their youth. Instead, he looked beyond their qualifications and expertise, focusing on the environmental conditions and the norms that emerged organically within each group.

The results? Shocking. The kindergartners, full of boundless curiosity and with little sense of norms, achieved incredible success. In contrast, the adults—many with advanced degrees—were burdened by their depth of knowledge and fear of failure. Most assumed that their increased experience and emotional maturity would have given the adults a leg up, but it didn't. So why were the kindergartners more successful?

The kindergartners showcased the Momentum Lever in action. Unlike their adult counterparts who often get entangled in the web of ego and status sensitivity, these young minds worked together seamlessly. They shared ideas openly, immediately put their ideas to the test or experiment right away, and were not afraid to make mistakes or see their idea not work, demonstrating the power of psychological safety and uninhibited participation in fostering innovation.

The success of the kindergartners reveals three key insights.

1. Environment Matters: Environmental conditions and the norms that shape behavior within teams greatly impact performance. What norms shape your team's behavior, and how does that influence performance?
2. A Posture of Progress: The kindergartners were champions of progress over perfection. They immediately converted their analysis into action, leveraging their learning to iterate on their latest prototype. They learned by doing, and they weren't afraid to make mistakes. Without the fear of failure and judgment weighing them down, each failed attempt simply became a prompt to try something new.
3. Navigating Today's Pace: Embracing the norms that proved successful for the kindergartners is no longer just advantageous—it's imperative. The ability to pivot quickly, learn from mistakes, and maintain a steadfast focus on progress has become the hallmark of winning teams.

As teams, we can learn a lot about Momentum by thinking more like kindergartners.

# A Tale of Two Teams

As we dive into the Momentum Lever, let's compare two teams as an illustration.

At Organization A, excellence isn't just a goal. It's the organization's known key differentiator and core to everything they do. From the onset, Jose, a new manager, realizes that every project, every presentation, and every report must not only meet but exceed the highest standards. This relentless pursuit of perfection creates an intense, high-pressure environment.

Staff meetings are less about recognizing progress and more about honoring great achievements and pointing out even the smallest flaws. Leaders are fixated on excellence—not small wins—and the bulk of the team's energy is consumed by perfecting details, often at the expense of moving forward. Jose notices the palpable tension among his colleagues. They are driven by the fear of not delivering exceptional results. This pressure leads to long hours, burnout, and stifled creativity.

While Organization A does occasionally showcase its excellence, it often comes at a cost. The company misses market opportunities and delays product launches as the quest for perfection overrides the need for timely action. The irony is evident: in striving for perfection, the organization often falls short of achieving its full potential.

At Organization B, Jane is quickly immersed in a culture that breathes "progress over perfection." In her first week, she witnesses the launch of a new product feature that isn't flawless but is functional and meets customer needs. The team's approach is to refine it based on real-world feedback, emphasizing practical learning over theoretical perfection.

The mantra "We learn by doing" is not just a slogan but a lived experience in Organization B. Jane sees this in action when a junior team member proposes an unconventional marketing strategy. Instead of dismissing it for its lack of polish, the team experiments with it on a small scale, garnering valuable insights and unexpected successes.

Regular "action meetings" (in Rhythm) are a staple, where the focus is on what steps to take next rather than dwelling on exhaustive analyses. Jane loves how these meetings end with clear action items, encouraging immediate implementation and continuous progress.

In this environment, feedback is given and received as a tool for growth, not criticism. Her team thrives under this model, confidently sharing ideas and learning from each other, driving the organization's momentum forward. Organization B is still focused on quality and excellent delivery, and they are valued alongside progress. They prioritize "progress over perfection," and they do so without compromising on quality.

The key difference between these two teams is their likelihood to find Momentum. Like so many modern organizations, Organization A is stuck in the status quo. Fear of failure looms in the background of every decision and discussion, making it hard for new ideas to take root. This fear of failure and reluctance to release imperfect work leads to a pervasive feeling of stuckness. When that feeling persists, it turns into apathy, and teams struggle to make any progress.

Organization B has embraced the spirit of Momentum, a desire to learn and grow through experimentation coupled with an unwillingness to stick with the status quo. Leaders actively encourage experimentation and learning from failure. As a result, they regularly feel a sense of progress in their work.

# How Do Teams Get So Stuck?

Have you been on a team like the one in Organization A? Many organizations function this way. The overarching feeling is stagnation—new ideas don't move, and everything functions the way it always has. People hope to develop new and better ways of working, but the idea of change feels so overwhelming and unlikely that they talk themselves out of it before they even try.

Typically, these teams overemphasize analysis. Analysis itself is not bad, but at times, it becomes an excuse not to take action, and it stalls progress. "Analysis paralysis" is a common phenomenon in teams where a new project or idea fails to launch because a leader or team insists on more and more data and analysis. Analysis and understanding consume too much time and energy at the expense of action and progress.

In *The Paradox of Choice: Why More Is Less*, Barry Schwartz explains that we increasingly have an endless array of choices. We tend to think that choice gives us fulfillment and freedom, but in reality, it makes it harder to arrive at a decision. As soon as we make a choice, we begin to wonder if we could have made a better one. This wondering ends up diminishing our pleasure. When we remember these experiences, it makes it even harder to make the next decision. Many people bring this mindset to the teams they work on, making it challenging to make group decisions.

Teams also commonly struggle with perfectionism, insisting on more revisions or updates or iterations in search of the perfect product rather than launching a product that's good enough. The challenge with perfectionism is that "perfect" does not exist, and after so many revisions, any change or update offers minor value compared to the high cost of time and missed opportunities due to the delay.

It can be challenging to identify a culture of perfectionism. Often, it masquerades as "Commitment to Excellence." It's hard to be the person on a team who stands up and says, "I think our pursuit of excellence is hurting our performance." Yet, it's important to see the connection between this espoused value and how a team can find themselves saddled with the type of pervasive perfectionism that stagnates momentum.

While harmful beliefs may not be documented anywhere, beneath the surface, you can find them guiding the behaviors of teams like the one in Organization A. Beliefs like:

- Detailed planning and strict adherence to plans are more important than responding to change.
- Finished products or projects must be perfect to be worth launching.
- Rigorous analysis is more important than progress and action.
- Learn first, then act. Know what you're doing before trying anything new.

For many people, we've been conditioned to fear failure and mistakes. From childhood, societal norms shape our behaviors and attitudes well into adulthood. In schools, the emphasis on perfect scores discourages risk-taking and reinforces the notion that we should be ashamed of our mistakes rather than embracing them as opportunities for learning.

The understandable and common result is to double down on caution. Unfortunately, this posture of fear limits progress and kills innovation. A compounding effect is at play here as well. As teams allow each individual to fear failure, the aggregate of the team is fear of failure. But as a team starts to tip the scale, embracing failure as a learning opportunity, it helps them learn, generating momentum.

Why do so many organizations live in this legacy state? The short answer is that their systems have been designed to work that way. We can see this stagnation show up in a variety of ways:

- Meetings fail to bring tension and inefficiency to the surface so they can be addressed, which hinders constructive dialogue and idea generation.
- The team is unfamiliar with experimenting and has no framework to try new ideas.
- The team overemphasizes analysis and excellence, stifling new and creative solutions and leading to a reluctance to take risks or pursue unconventional ideas.
- The team views highly impactful organizational processes as fixed and "the way it works here," discouraging suggestions for improvement.
- The unspoken preference for maintaining the status quo stifles free and creative thinking, perpetuating a culture of complacency and resistance to change.
- New ideas can only advance if they have survived multiple rounds of vetting.

For teams to succeed in the dynamic world of work today, they need to embrace momentum, the new spirit of work.

## The New Spirit of Work

As we were creating the 6 Levers framework, we had many animated debates about what dimensions of organizational health should and should not be considered a key Lever. Our essential criteria for each Lever were:

1. That it was a core and macro indicator of team health
2. That it could be systematically engineered and put into practice.

For a while, we considered the Momentum Lever to simply be the "spirit" of the organizational operating system rather than being its own distinct Lever. That was because we believed that a spirit of momentum or a team's posture of progress and default toward learning and experimentation is one that must run through the adoption of every Lever as well as the broader change effort a team undertakes when they set out to design and adopt a more intentional org OS. While this is certainly true—that Momentum is the new spirit of work—we decided it was also an essential Lever to the framework because of its importance to organizational health and the fact that it can be systematically harnessed through specific tools and practices.

What does a team look like that has embraced the spirit of Momentum? It starts with learning to replace old norms of working with a new mindsets and practices that enable them to sustain their spirit of Momentum for the long term.

| Old Norms & Practices | New Norms & Practices |
|---|---|
| Limit risk to avoid mistakes and judgment | It's safe to make mistakes |
| Results are all that matters | Learning is just as important as results |
| Commitment to excellence | Progress over perfection |
| We value rigorous analysis | We learn by doing |

In the previous section, we talked about the symptoms of organizational stagnation. But what if, instead, a team embraced new mindsets for this new spirit of work? Consider these scenarios:

- Instead of conflict-averse meeting dynamics, the team structures their meetings to build in time to address emergent issues,

encourage open communication, and directly address tensions and inefficiencies.
- To help overcome a fear of trying new things, the team establishes a culture of experimentation and iterative solution development with a way to celebrate progress and learn from both successes and failures.
- Instead of analysis paralysis, the team encourages a culture of action by promoting mantras like "good enough for now" rather than perfectionism, setting clear deadlines for decision-making and fostering an environment where calculated risks are encouraged and celebrated.
- Instead of inflexible processes, the team fosters a culture of continuous improvement by actively seeking feedback from employees, enabling teams to challenge existing processes in a routine and systematic way, and adopting lean practices for piloting and implementing new ideas.
- To overcome resistance to change, the team encourages open dialogue about the need for change, providing opportunities for employees to voice concerns and contribute ideas and recognizing and rewarding individuals and teams that champion innovation and embrace new ways of working.

All this becomes possible when a team harnesses the power of Momentum.

## The Momentum Equation

To understand the power of momentum within teams, consider the scientific formula: Momentum = Mass x Velocity. This mathematical equation models the unique variables impacting progress and dynamism within a team. In physics, momentum is defined as the product of an object's mass and velocity, signifying the quantity of motion it possesses. Similarly, within organizations, momentum can be understood as the collective force generated by a team's combined efforts and its speed of progress.

In physics, momentum drives motion and change. Within organizations, momentum fuels productivity, change, progress, and even employee engagement. Momentum embodies the spirit of continuous improvement and proactive action, which are essential for organizational success. In the formula, mass represents the collective understanding and application of the value of momentum by each team member. It signifies the depth of commitment and engagement within the team, reflecting the combined energy and effort directed toward common goals. Velocity symbolizes the speed and direction at which the team progresses. It represents the agility and responsiveness of the team, their ability to adapt to changing circumstances, and the pace at which they move toward their objectives.

Together, mass and velocity form the core components of Momentum within organizations, driving progress and fostering a culture of continuous improvement. Harnessing Momentum has incredible power to increase effectiveness and team health for a number of reasons.

## Momentum Is Liberating

When a team embraces Momentum, it can feel freeing. Whereas previously, the team felt caged in by a fear of failure, now they have permission to try new things, experiment, and iterate. In *Linchpin: Are You Indispensable?,* Seth Godin describes "shipping" as a mindset that encourages individuals to move from planning and ideation to actual execution and contribution. When teams embrace a shipping mindset, they learn through doing and more easily see their progress. When that happens, they can find the type of Momentum that feels unstoppable.

## Teams Feel Hope Again

In a team stuck in stagnation, it can feel hopeless that anything will ever change. As teams start to practice Momentum, they begin to see small wins. These incremental gains might feel insignificant, but don't be fooled. These are the first signs of Momentum taking hold. As the small wins accrue, teams will feel hope that change is possible, even when the task at hand feels insurmountable.

By fueling these wins and achievements, Momentum reinforces the team's belief in its abilities. This positive reinforcement is vital for maintaining morale and motivation.

## Teams Can Overcome Inertia

As teams start to take action, it helps to build up enough momentum—in the scientific sense—to overcome the great sense of inertia in an organization. At the start of any new initiative, teams are likely to face some resistance, and as their Momentum gains strength, they'll be better equipped to overcome the obstacles. Once a team is in motion, it becomes easier to sustain and build upon that movement as the team benefits from two forces: 1) momentum and engagement, and 2) adaptation and learning.

- Motivation and engagement: Achieving early successes and building momentum provides a sense of achievement, boosting team morale and motivation. When individuals see progress, they are more likely to be engaged and committed to the overall strategic vision.
- Adaptation and learning: Momentum allows teams to adapt and learn from their experiences. It provides an opportunity for continuous improvement, enabling teams to refine their strategies based on real-world feedback and changing circumstances.

Teams can start to build Momentum by embracing several key practices.

# The Practice of Momentum

One important note before diving in: for your practice of Momentum to be effective, your team must have a foundation of team psychological safety (which we touched on in Chapter 7: Cohesion). If teams jump into trying to improve their ways of working without tending to the trust needed to do so, they run a significant risk of doing more harm than good.

Without psychological safety, it's hard to embrace "progress over perfection," engage in honest feedback, or fully embrace a "we learn by doing" attitude. A team needs that foundation of trust to feel comfortable shifting into a mindset of risk-taking and mistake-making.

In a team culture that's highly dysfunctional or toxic, these practices are highly unlikely to find traction and, even worse, they could be harmful. For example, if an employee has been publicly called out by a colleague for making a mistake, embracing "learn by doing" may not make sense until the team has done work to build psychological safety and change the norm about making mistakes.

For those eager to begin embracing the spirit of Momentum, you can start with three key intentional practices. While they are relatively simple to understand, we call them practices because they will take just that to become habits.

> **Three Practices to Build Momentum**
>
> 1. Build a culture of feedback
> 2. Limit work in progress
> 3. Embrace small wins

Consider them not just guidelines but also adaptable tools, empowering you to experiment and adjust as you learn what's working best for your team.

# Create a Culture of Feedback

The unfortunate reality for many individuals is that feedback often becomes synonymous with annual performance reviews or the initiation of a performance improvement plan. The mere mention of feedback tends to evoke images of delivering negative critiques, a task seen as requiring tremendous courage, often dissuading individuals from engaging in it altogether.

However, when feedback becomes an integral part of a team's operating rhythm, it is normalized, thoughtful, widely shared, multidirectional, and, most importantly, expected. Given that many of us have experienced environments where feedback is a rare occurrence, creating a culture that normalizes it takes a good deal of intention. Teams can focus on three foundational building blocks to construct a robust culture of feedback: normalizing precise praise, learning how to request feedback, and establishing feedback systems that integrate it into everyday practices.

**The ideal ratio of precise praise to constructive feedback should be four or even five to one.** This balance builds trust, making recipients more receptive to constructive feedback. However, authenticity is crucial. Refrain from manufacturing positive feedback merely to segue into the more critical points, as this can be perceived as insincere and counterproductive.

Instead, consider the ratio as a holistic measure across the entire relationship. Then, it won't feel necessary to offer a compliment sandwich every time you share constructive feedback. Moreover, don't overlook the precision aspect of positive feedback. Instead of a generic "Great job on that presentation today," try, "When you led the exercise about asking people to draft examples of precise praise, the group was engaged, and the learning clicked. Awesome job there!"

Another essential aspect of fostering a robust culture of feedback is actively seeking it. When team members know you are actively seeking specific feedback, it becomes easier for them to give feedback. Being specific in your requests and narrowing the focus of the feedback you're looking for helps the giver focus and opens the door to broader feedback opportunities in the relationship.

To embed the habit of regular feedback, build feedback systems into your team's rhythms and practices. Involve as many team members as possible in the design to ensure shared ownership and belief in the systems. Examples of feedback systems include one-on-one sessions, a "feedback tracker," rituals for public precise praise, Agreements for delivering constructive feedback, and a feedback guide connecting organizational tenets to feedback practices—a valuable tool for onboarding and training.

Teams intentionally building a culture of feedback are more likely to gain Momentum. In such a culture, teams can swiftly adapt, pivoting away from ineffective ideas and navigating conflicts in their early stages before escalation. A culture of feedback embraces a "small and often" mindset, a departure from the "big and rare" approach seen in annual reviews or infrequent 360-degree assessments. In the "small and often" paradigm, feedback flows continuously, precise praise becomes a routine occurrence, and constructive feedback, even on minor matters, is anchored in trust and a belief in the best in each other.

## Limit Work in Progress

Generating new ideas isn't usually the hurdle for most teams. The challenge lies in selecting which ideas to focus on. This struggle often leads to an overload of work as teams, attempting to juggle multiple projects, end up being unrealistic about their capacity. Engaging in a multitude of "important" projects makes it exceedingly difficult to build and sustain Momentum. Just as a glimmer of progress appears, the need to switch tasks interrupts the flow, hindering a sense that anything will ever reach completion.

In the realm of agile development, a widely recognized mantra advises teams to "stop starting and start finishing." The allure of shiny new projects often entices teams to initiate fresh endeavors before concluding existing ones. This tendency not only creates bottlenecks and inefficiencies but also fosters a pervasive feeling that teams won't ever feel a sense of progress.

The concept of Work in Progress (WIP) revolves around the volume of work a team can realistically complete within a specific timeframe. Limiting WIP aligns with the Essentialist mindset that by focusing on fewer tasks, we can achieve more and generate Momentum.

Among the various inhibitors to Momentum caused by excessive WIP, the cost of context switching is most significant. In the book *Attention Span* by Gloria Mark, Professor of Informatics at UC Irvine, she reveals that regaining focus after even a brief interruption—like a "quick question" via Slack—takes an average of more than twenty-three minutes. Our minds linger on the previous task as we transition to a new one. Each task switch diminishes the likelihood of regaining focus, resulting in a sense of spinning in place rather than forward momentum. Teams that embrace the practice of limiting WIP can significantly increase their chances of making meaningful progress on their most crucial work.

Given the dynamic nature of teamwork, it's crucial to acknowledge that the journey toward limiting WIP is an iterative process. Continuous improvement is not just a concept; it's a practice that requires teams to regularly reflect on their workflows and adapt strategies. By cultivating a mindset that values learning from experiences, teams can refine their approaches, identify patterns of success, and mitigate challenges over time. The journey toward optimizing WIP is not a one-time fix but an ongoing commitment to efficiency and effectiveness. In embracing this mindset, teams navigate the pitfalls of excessive WIP and create a culture that continually refines its processes, unlocking sustained momentum and progress.

## Embrace Small Wins

Shaun worked with a couple of organizations that addressed homelessness, and he can attest to the fact that it's a complex and challenging issue, often requiring extensive resources and the participation of many stakeholders to move the needle and see progress at a community level.

Shaun's church is located in an urban area where the problem of homelessness is visible. Recently, he led a course at the church for fellow church members who wanted to learn about the problem of homelessness and explore ways to make a difference. He was struck that each individual started the class with a sense of overwhelm about where to begin, but by the end, they felt hope.

At the outset, they could only see how big of a problem it was, but the class broke this norm as they learned more about the causes of homelessness. By the end, they understood what they could do about it, however small. They left with a sense of hope and knowledge about how to take a step forward.

The class was designed to deepen understanding at the personal and systems levels. With that increased understanding, Shaun asked them to take one step forward. The facilitators presented the class with three actions they could take. After everyone chose one of the actions, everyone gathered one last time for a brainstorming session about how the church could better engage members in addressing homelessness in the neighborhood. The ideas were flowing, and hope abounded. Within six weeks, people who had felt overwhelmed now felt a strong sense of how they could make a difference.

In the face of major challenges that feel intractable, if we focus on what we can do, however small, we can accrue small wins and build Momentum that enables us to address larger and larger challenges as we go. When a few wins start stacking together, teams will feel the incredible force of Momentum.

## But, Momentum Toward What?

"Unsure of our direction, we often double our pace."

Alan Briggs, a leadership coach and backcountry exploration guide, shared this truth with Josh: The backcountry yields horror stories of people getting lost, sometimes for days. When we're unsure, we want to get there sooner. So we speed up—in the wrong direction.

This happens with teams, too. Momentum is critical for teams to feel like they're making progress. In the Momentum Lever, we teach teams that "progress is fuel," "progress over perfection," and "learn by doing." Each of these principles helps teams overcome analysis paralysis and keep moving.

But this speed doesn't do us any good if we're headed in the wrong direction.

To embrace the true power of Momentum, we must root it in Identity and Focus. If a team isn't clear on their Identity and Focus and they start to go faster, they run the risk of getting further and further off course.

Maybe a team is developing a new program or product. They iterate and make changes daily (or even hourly) as they accelerate toward the launch date. To make sure they stay on course and don't devolve into total chaos, they check in weekly to revisit their Focus. They ask, "Are we hitting our goals? Are we pointed in the right direction?" They offer feedback to each other and create space for learning.

It's this combination of Momentum with Identity and Focus that ensures that when we're moving, we're moving in the right direction.

### Recap of the Momentum Lever

The Momentum Lever accelerates progress, learning, and continuous improvement, and it strengthens a culture of vulnerability and engagement. A team with strong Momentum has tools, practices, and habits to give effective feedback and to spend dedicated time on reflection and learning from past projects.

**Questions for Reflection**

1. Does your team feel willing to take chances and try new ideas?
2. Does your organization have a strong culture of feedback?
3. Does your team regularly carve out time to reflect and learn from your experiences?
4. Out of all 6 Levers, does strengthening Momentum seem like one of the priorities for your organization?

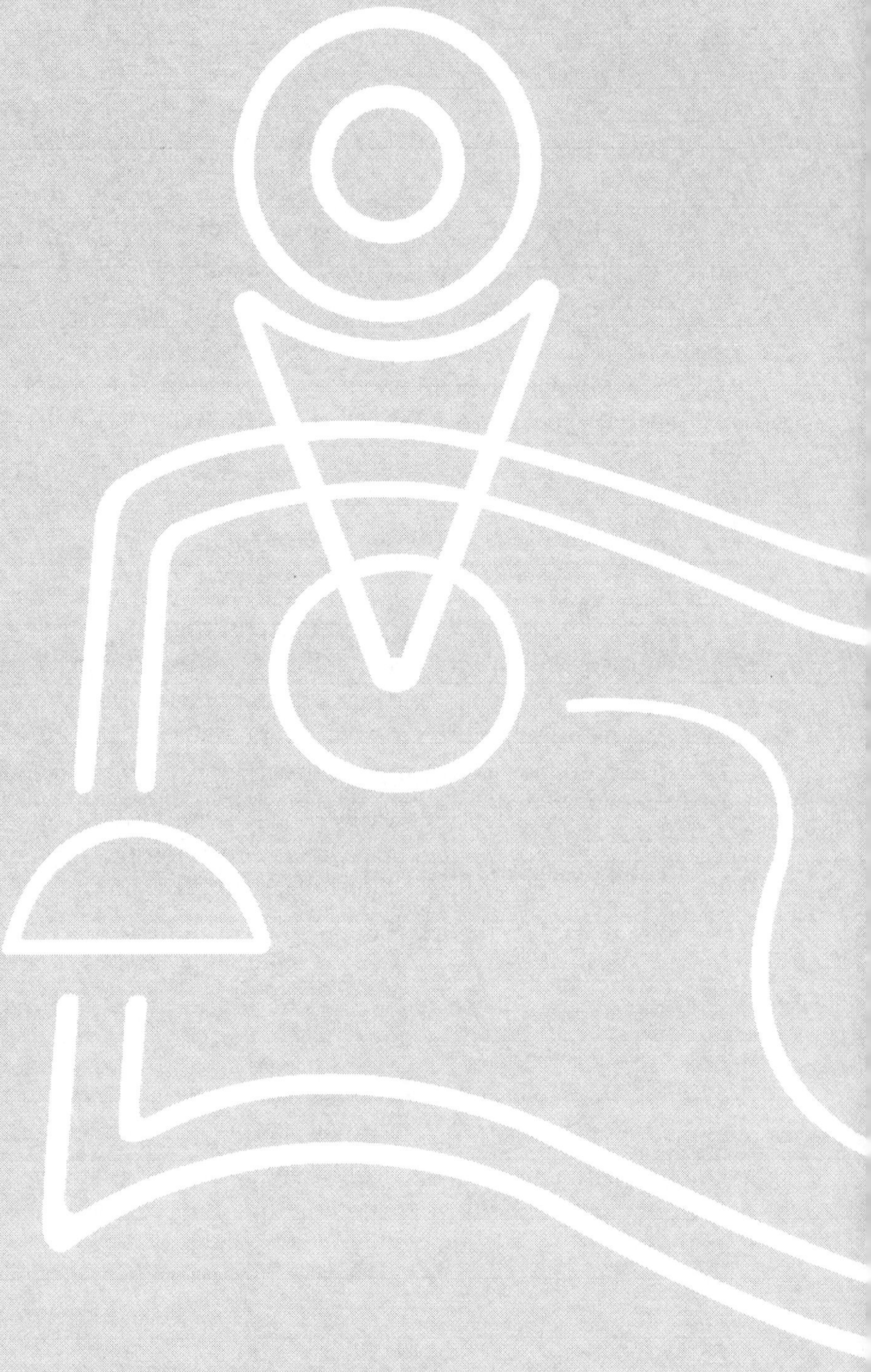

# Getting Started

We live in a world that constantly tells us there are only two outcomes: winning or losing. As a result, it can be hard to see the progress we are making.

About six months into working with an organization, Shaun had a conversation with the CEO. She'd just completed her first quarter with a clear set of quarterly priorities, wrapping it up with a Quarterly Sync to reflect on the previous quarter and set priorities for the next one.

Shaun asked how the Quarterly Sync went, and she gave him an unenthusiastic "Okay."

"Why did it go 'Okay?'" he asked.

She mentioned several ways the meeting could have gone better, such as they could have accomplished more of their priorities, and she could have facilitated the meeting better.

He asked, "But this is the first time y'all have had short-term priorities, right? You've never had an aligned set of goals that you worked on as a team and monitored together, have you?"

She said no.

"Well, that's awesome," he told her. "You did that for the first time, and the fact that you had a set of quarterly priorities to monitor for the first time feels like meaningful progress to me."

"I guess you're right," she said.

"And this was your first time facilitating a Quarterly Sync for your team, wasn't it?"

"Yeah."

"Do you feel like you'll probably do it better next time based on the experience of jumping in and doing it this time?"

"Yes, I do," she confirmed.

"That's great progress that you made. You jumped in and did it. The key is in learning by doing, and you did that."

As leaders, we tend to only see what could have been better, and we miss the progress we have made. Many leaders tell themselves they're not doing well enough, but they're making incredible progress that they can't see.

Shaun's encouragement to that leader—and to you as you embark on this journey—is to jump in and get started, learn by doing, and celebrate the small wins as they come.

We've got guidance to share on how to do just that.

## Start Small

When contemplating ideas as significant as organization- or team-wide changes, our initial thoughts often veer to the necessity of big leaps. It's a common belief: to achieve monumental success, monumental change is essential. This belief often keeps teams from starting at all. It can feel overwhelming when they consider all the work already in front of them. However, this perspective misses a crucial point: sometimes, we need to think small.

As James Clear articulates in his exploration of habit formation, transformation often occurs in small, consistent increments. It's these step-by-step changes that accumulate over time that lead to substantial shifts. Don't underestimate the power of small changes. As teams start to notice and celebrate these little wins, momentum builds.

These small wins not only propel the team toward greater progress but also play a crucial role in swaying the skeptics. Witnessing tangible improvement—however small—rallies support and fosters a shared belief in the change process.

Here's an example of a team taking a small step to make progress toward what felt like a significant problem. A leadership team at one of the organizations we were supporting had grown quite frustrated with the effectiveness of their meetings. This team of five people realized that they rarely had time to collaboratively and synchronously work through urgent and important issues. All their existing meeting Rhythms were designed to work through predetermined agenda items. While the meetings did serve the purpose of alignment on key updates, they left no space for discussion of important, emergent issues. So, the team redesigned one of their weekly meetings to save at least half of the meeting time to work through emergent issues of the week.

As they implemented this new Rhythm, the team began to feel a sense of relief. As big issues arose throughout the week, the team knew they were always only a few days away from being able to bring the issue to the whole team. Whereas before, discussion was limited to one-on-one side conversations that often siloed key information, but now, the team had a built-in space to work through important and emergent issues.

This one change to one meeting gave the team hope that they could redesign other recurring Rhythms to be more effective. This approach, focusing on incremental improvements executed with consistency, instills a sense of possibility and opens up a new world of experimentation and growth. It demonstrates that the journey to widespread organizational health doesn't necessarily require sweeping, immediate transformations but that it can be effectively achieved through a series of small, deliberate steps.

Think of designing your org OS like rehabbing a house while living in it, taking it one room at a time. You might start with the second bathroom, then a bedroom, then the kitchen, prioritizing each room based on where you are most excited to see the transformation and what you have the capacity to work on. Working in every room at once while living in the house would disrupt your life and make you miserable. The same is true for designing your org OS: take it one piece at a time.

# How Do We Start?

Taking on the task of intentionally designing your org OS can feel monumental and intimidating. The reality is that your team's current situation is unique. You're facing challenges today that are likely different than if you had read this book a year ago. We have ideas on how you can get started and gain Momentum.

## Choose a Navigator

To get your team running on 6 Levers, a pivotal factor is the presence of an internal lead or point person who enthusiastically takes charge of coordinating the details to prioritize, experiment, and reflect thoughtfully on each change implemented by the team as it relates to the org OS.

While it's customary for teams to appoint leaders for various facets of their work, the concept may initially seem unfamiliar when applied to their org OS. This key individual—what we call the Navigator—plays a vital role in steering the course of systems innovation and adaptation within the team, providing a guiding hand through the uncharted waters of change.

Navigators are primarily responsible for leading the development and implementation of 6 Levers on a team. They are the lead coordinators, facilitators, and champions of the team's org OS. Oftentimes, organizations begin implementing 6 Levers with the executive team. Small organizations with only one or two teams probably need only one Navigator. For organizations with hundreds or thousands of people, it's important to define the core teams and then determine a Navigator for each core team. Each core team will have important differentiated contexts, cultures, and goals that require them to have autonomy in designing their team's org OS.

The Navigator role includes design and strategy, facilitation and training, and follow-through and continuous improvement.

### Characteristics of a Great Navigator

- **Systems thinkers:** Navigators are curious about how different parts of a system influence each other and try to see the upstream causes to get to the root.

- **Growth-oriented and open-minded:** Navigators are open to new ideas and constantly look to grow as individuals and as a team. They bring a spirit of curiosity and experimentation as they implement different pieces of the framework.

- **Passionate about organizational health and people:** Navigators are excited about the opportunity to lead their teams to greater health without sacrificing results—or their team's well-being—in the process.

- **Natural collaborators:** Navigators must work across teams, sometimes without direct authority. They need to communicate clearly and collaborate well to pave the way for change to happen.

- **Doers:** Navigators need to be action-oriented, organized, and efficient to move things forward and keep the team rowing in the same direction.

Identifying and empowering each team's Navigator helps ensure you don't leave the design of your org OS to chance. It also communicates how important it is to bring resources and attention to intentionally designing the way you work. Lastly, in addition to the benefits it will bring the team, it can be a powerful way to empower and develop systems thinkers who are eager to design better ways of working.

## Assess Where You Are

We designed the framework so teams could begin running on 6 Levers by jumping into any one of the Levers. The first step is to choose a Lever, then choose a practice or tool within that Lever.

How do you decide which Lever to begin with? Get together with your team and think through the following questions.

### Where Do We Stand?

Run through this quick self-assessment to help your team think about your capability within each Lever. Use this data as a starting point for conversations with your team as you move on to the next section.

## Organizational Health Self-Assessment

Answer each question, either as a team or by yourself. Look for areas where you scored a 1 or 2, and consider starting your 6 Levers journey there.

1. I feel a strong sense of clarity and connection to our organization's purpose, beliefs, values, and key indicators of success (Identity Lever).

   Strongly Agree  **1  2  3  4  5**  Strongly Disagree

2. Leadership is a clear strength across all members of our team (Leadership Lever).

   Strongly Agree  **1  2  3  4  5**  Strongly Disagree

3. Our team has clear annual goals and has a discipline of creating focus on the most important things across the organization (Focus Lever).

   Strongly Agree  **1  2  3  4  5**  Strongly Disagree

4. Our team feels healthy and cohesive. We work well together and have effective ways to resolve conflict (Cohesion Lever).

   Strongly Agree  **1  2  3  4  5**  Strongly Disagree

5. Our team has effective habits, and our meetings are productive and engaging (Rhythm Lever).

   Strongly Agree  **1  2  3  4  5**  Strongly Disagree

6. Our team is action-oriented and consistently moves strategic work forward (Momentum Lever).

   Strongly Agree  **1  2  3  4  5**  Strongly Disagree

## Where's the Energy?

What area does your team currently feel most compelled to improve? Is it your weekly team meeting? Start with Rhythm. Is it clarity around setting priorities? Begin with Focus. Is it more navigating tension among team members? Cohesion is a great place to start. Go with the energy, even if it doesn't feel like your most burning issue. This approach will help build Momentum.

## What's Our Capacity?

How much capacity does your team currently have to engage meaningfully in driving this change? If you are in a busier season, you might try a micro change. If you have more capacity, you can take on more. Regardless of where you think you are, lean into engineering success as you begin. Don't pick the most challenging aspect of your teamwork. Build up your org OS design muscles first with easier initiatives.

# Start Building the Foundation

Based on your self-assessment, energy, and capacity, pick one or two parts of the 6 Levers framework to begin working on. Let's revisit some of those foundational requirements of an org OS that we introduced in Chapter 1 and connect them to the 6 Levers. The best way to approach the following table is to think of these system requirements as the beginning of your journey to bring more intention to your org OS. This isn't meant to be an exhaustive list of requirements but rather a way to help you gain Momentum as your organization or team begins to leverage the power of bringing intention to your org OS.

While all organizations will benefit from having these foundational pieces in place, you may find that you need to address an issue outside of this list before getting all these foundational pieces in place. That could absolutely be the right call. Include your team in discerning where to start, and pay attention to where the motivation is. For example, a team that has struggled to navigate recurring conflict might decide to elevate conflict resolution training and associated Agreements to make progress there. This team might rightfully decide this is one of the first aspects of their org OS that they want to work on, and if the motivation is there, they should feel empowered to go for it.

Regardless of where you start, know that you will find designing your org OS easier once you have these foundational pieces in place. A team that has adopted a way to set and adjust priorities can leverage that process to systematically improve other aspects of their org OS. For example, someone on a team might raise a concern about people feeling unequipped to give feedback. If that team has a way to set Quarterly Priorities, they could use that process to bring focus to the issue in a quarter. If they don't have a way to set, monitor, and adjust team priorities, they might struggle to find Momentum in addressing the issue.

GETTING STARTED

## Building the Foundation

| System Requirement | Related Lever(s) | Action |
|---|---|---|
| Clearly defined organizational identity | Identity | ▪ Build a Compass that defines and clarifies each of the following: beliefs, mission, Theory of Impact, vitals, values, and tenets |
| A routine way to define and set targets for key performance measures | Identity, Focus, and Rhythm | ▪ Establish vitals<br>▪ Set targets for each one<br>▪ Monitor and discuss progress |
| A systematic approach to leadership development | Leadership | ▪ Define your core Leadership Competencies, such as self-awareness, curiosity, or vulnerability<br>▪ Establish an approach to leadership development, such as regular training, coaching, and learning opportunities for existing and emerging leaders throughout the organization |
| An adopted approach to strategic planning | Focus | ▪ Establish a three- to five-year vision<br>▪ Set annual goals<br>▪ Get in the practice of setting short-term priorities each quarter or semester |
| A methodology for setting and monitoring organizational and team priorities, both long term and short term | Focus | ▪ Adopt an Operating Cycle, including an Annual Sync, Quarterly or Semester Sync, and a weekly or bi-weekly Leadership Team Meeting |

## Building the Foundation

| System Requirement | Related Lever(s) | Action |
|---|---|---|
| Defined Operating Cycle consisting of strategic Annual and Quarterly Syncs | Rhythm | - Operating Cycle including Annual Sync, Quarterly Sync |
| Clearly established communication norms | Cohesion and Rhythm | - Communication Agreements Communication Rhythms, both synchronous and asynchronous |
| Well-designed meeting structures across teams | Rhythm | - Rhythm design including clear objectives for recurring meetings and agendas developed to achieve them |
| Established and shared norms and protocols for conflict resolution | Cohesion | - Complete training focused on building trust, psychological safety, and engagement<br>Use the Agreements tool to streamline tension resolution and continuous improvement |

## Consider the interconnections

As you decide where to start, consider the interconnected nature of your org OS. For example, you could start in the Focus Lever and set one-year goals, but those goals might feel more meaningful if you have first clarified your Identity and can consider your vitals as you develop them. Similarly, you could work to strengthen Cohesion by adopting a few working Agreements, but that process might feel stronger if you first establish a Rhythm to monitor and review them. As evidenced in the table, some system requirements necessitate teams accessing multiple Levers.

## Monitor and Review

Build in space in one of your recurring team meetings to review progress. When you decide your starting point, choose a checkpoint to reflect, adapt, and share learning. Based on what you learn in that conversation, agree on a next step to either continue making improvements in that area or move on to another part of our system. The key here is creating the space to reflect and learn.

◆ ◆ ◆

Ultimately, running on 6 Levers is not a strict playbook with a beginning and an end. It's a continuous, flowing journey, and these steps will help you gain Momentum.

# Let's Go

As you begin to run on 6 Levers, keep in mind that it's an adaptive, iterative process. No two organizations will run 6 Levers the same way. Take the framework and make it your own. It's an art that requires creative thinking and experimentation. As you work through different Levers, practices, and tools, some will work immediately, and some will need tweaking to make them fit your team's unique culture.

For more ideas, guidance, and training, or to hire a guide, visit www.6levers.co.

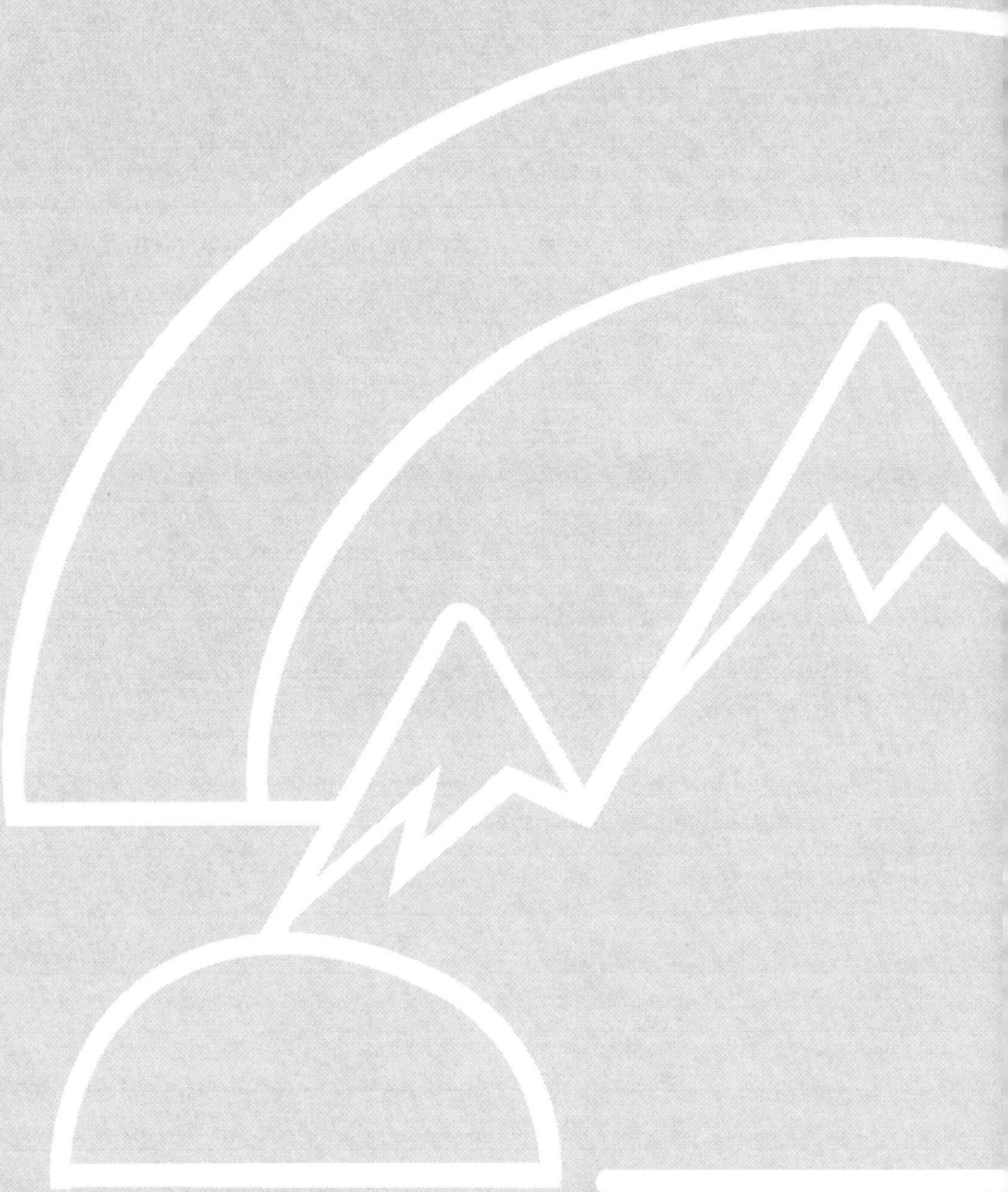

It's a Journey

The energy was high as the Jamaican bobsled team headed to their final race in the 1988 Winter Olympics. They were coming from a tropical country to compete in a snow sport, and no one believed the team would make it far, but this resilient group exceeded expectations and was in the running for a medal.

As depicted in the 1993 movie *Cool Runnings*, the crowd was tense with excitement and anticipation as the Jamaican team began the race. They started strong, but when a blade came loose in the team's rickety sled, the Jamaicans careened off course, overturning short of the finish line.

It's a dramatic couple of seconds as they realize they've lost. The crowd appeared to hold its breath, waiting to see what the Jamaican team would do as the disappointment gripped everyone in the stadium and those watching on television. But instead of giving up, the team got back on their feet, hoisted the sled on their shoulders, and carried it across the finish line to a chorus of cheers and congratulations. Their many detractors became supporters—even the competitors.

## It's a Journey

What we learn from *Cool Runnings* is that the journey is just as important as winning the race. In the end, how we go about the journey and how we feel throughout it has a greater impact on us than the final result of what we're trying to achieve. The Jamaican team didn't win the Olympics, but in the end, it's their process and experience—and the intangible outcomes generated throughout the journey—that proved to be just as impactful as winning the race. In addition to getting close to winning a medal, they:

- Grew as a team and formed lasting relationships
- Strengthened their own beliefs and sense of possibility
- Proved to themselves what they were capable of

- Galvanized a nation of supporters
- Inspired the world

Our hope in developing the 6 Levers framework is to make a more meaningful journey possible for you. Even more than supporting the achievement of any business goal, the framework is designed to enable a thriving workplace—an environment where the journey is as meaningful as the destination.

# Where Everyone Can Thrive

As a framework with humans at its heart, we believe in working to create workplaces where anyone can thrive. By implementing an organizational operating framework that promotes inclusion and collaboration, organizations can create a more meaningful work environment. 6 Levers helps in five major ways.

1. **Increases Clarity on How Work Works:** The framework empowers team members by providing them with a common platform to contribute and engage. By shining a light on how work works, shared systems and language create an environment that makes it much easier for anyone to influence and positively impact organizational culture. It can go a long way in eliminating the dynamic where only a few key people truly understand the way key systems are developed and upheld.
2. **Strengthens Buy-in with Democratized Design:** When designing a team's OS, we believe that each member of the team should have a voice in creating the system. When every member of a team can design how they work with each other, it creates a sense that they can navigate any problem that comes their way.
3. **Establishes Fair and Transparent Ways of Working:** The framework promotes fairness and transparency because the norms, practices, and routines regarding the way work works are defined and available for the team to see. When all team

members operate within the same set of rules, guidelines, and expectations, it reduces the likelihood of unnecessary tension.
4. **Demystifies Decision-Making:** The framework promotes effective communication and information-sharing across team members, regardless of their position within the team. By actively involving all members in decision-making processes, shared systems and language create a sense of ownership and belonging. Team Agreements about their org OS should be known and accessible to anyone. That certainly includes Agreements about how decisions are made.
5. **Encourages Learning and Growth:** 6 Levers empowers people to acquire new skills and expand their capabilities through shared knowledge, resources, and tools. Keeping people and systems at the heart of work includes bringing intentionality to how people are developed, focusing on helping them access resources and support that allow them to learn and grow. In this reality, development is happening regularly, not just one or two times a year.

# At the Heart of Work

What if we flip the question? "What's the cost of not intentionally developing your organizational operating system?"

Burnout and turnover will continue. Too many people will miss the opportunity to be the leader they could be, and they will miss their chance to do their best work. Teams won't realize the potential only possible through highly collaborative and engaged environments. People will be barely present at both work and home.

Too many of us have resigned ourselves to the idea that work will be a place that only takes from us, but it has tremendous potential to be a source of goodness in our lives.

People and systems are at the heart of work. People infuse life into the systems they operate, while systems provide the structure and support for people to thrive. Together, they form the dynamic essence of organizational culture, propelling it toward success and innovation.

To create enduring organizational health, we must recognize the relationship between people and systems and nurture both in harmony. Neglecting one at the expense of the other leads to imbalance and frustration, hindering the organization's ability to adapt and evolve in a rapidly evolving world.

This means designing our systems both with and for people. *With people* means bringing people along to collaboratively design how work works. *For people* means that we design our systems with the needs of people at the center.

We believe organizations can transform to be places where people are engaged in work that is life-giving, not life-draining. Where people go to work every day, understanding the greater purpose they're working toward. Where people know that those they work with care about them and their needs. We believe sustainable health is possible—for our teams, our organizations, and ourselves. And it all begins at the heart of work.

# Notes

## 1. People and Systems

- Collins, James C. *Good to Great: Why Some Companies Make the Leap … and Others Don't*. HarperBusiness, 2001.
- Heath, Dan. *Upstream: The Quest to Solve Problems Before They Happen*. Simon & Schuster, 2020.

## 3. Identity

- Achor, Shawn, Andrew Reece, Gabriella Rosen Kellerman, and Alexi Robichaux. "9 Out of 10 People Are Willing to Earn Less Money to Do More-Meaningful Work." *Harvard Business Review*, November 6, 2018. https://hbr.org/2018/11/9-out-of-10-people-are-willing-to-earn-less-money-to-do-more-meaningful-work.
- Warby Parker. "History." Warby Parker. Accessed May 8, 2024. https://www.warbyparker.com/history.
- Five to Nine. "A Clear View on Culture: How Warby Parker Innovates on Employee Experience." *Medium*, March 22, 2019. https://medium.com/@info_37650/a-clear-view-on-culture-how-warby-parker-innovates-on-employee-experience-9410097ffaea.
- Joly, Hubert. "How to Connect Employees to Your Company's Purpose." *Harvard Business Review*. October 26, 2023. https://hbr.org/2023/10/how-to-connect-employees-to-your-companys-purpose.
- Clear, James. *Atomic Habits: An Easy & Proven Way to Build Good Habits & Break Bad Ones*. Avery, an imprint of Penguin Random House, 2018.

- Lencioni, Patrick. *The Advantage: Why Organizational Health Trumps Everything Else in Business.* Jossey-Bass, 2012.
- Kaplan, Robert S., and David P. Norton. "The Office of Strategy Management." *Harvard Business Review*, October 2005. https://hbr.org/2005/10/the-office-of-strategy-management.

## 4. Leadership

- Minor, Dylan, and Jan Rivkin. "Truly Human Leadership at Barry-Wehmiller." Harvard Business School Case 717-420, September 2016.
- Harter, Jim. "In New Workplace, U.S. Employee Engagement Stagnates." Gallup, January 23, 2024. https://www.gallup.com/workplace/608675/new-workplace-employee-engagement-stagnates.aspx.
- Edmondson, Amy. Interview with Dave Stachowiak, *Coaching for Leaders Podcast*, podcast audio, January 22, 2024. https://coachingforleaders.com/podcast/grow-from-your-errors-amy-edmondson/.
- "How DeMeco Ryans of 49ers became prime NFL head-coach candidate." *Sports News Inc.* January 19, 2023. https://sportsnewsinc.com/2023/01/19/how-demeco-ryans-of-49ers-became-prime-nfl-head-coach-candidate/.
- Eurich, Tasha. *Insight: Why We're Not As Self-aware As We Think, and How Seeing Ourselves Clearly Helps Us Succeed At Work and in Life.* Crown Business, 2017.
- Brown, Brené. *The Power of Vulnerability* [Video]. TED Conferences, June 2010. https://www.ted.com/talks/brene_brown_the_power_of_vulnerability?showsSubtitleTooltip=true&language=en.
- Morgan, Jacob. *Leading with Vulnerability: Unlock Your Greatest Superpower to Transform Yourself, Your Team, and Your Organization.* John Wiley & Sons, 2024.

- Duhigg, Charles. "What Google Learned from Its Quest to Build the Perfect Team." *The New York Times Magazine*, February 25, 2016. https://www.nytimes.com/2016/02/28/magazine/what-google-learned-from-its-quest-to-build-the-perfect-team.html.
- Gartner. "Successful Organizational Change Management: Reality or Aspiration?" Accessed May 8, 2024. https://www.gartner.com/en/human-resources/insights/organizational-change-management.
- Senge, Peter M. *The Fifth Discipline: The Art & Practice of the Learning Organization*. Doubleday, 2006.
- Pitonyak, John, and Rob Desimone. "How to Engage Frontline Managers." Gallup. Last updated January 19, 2024. https://www.gallup.com/workplace/395210/engage-frontline-managers.aspx.
- Pointer, Lindsey, and Kathleen McGoey. "Needs and Feelings Iceberg." Restorative Teaching Tools. Accessed May 8, 2024. https://restorativeteachingtools.com/wp-content/uploads/2020/10/Needs-and-Feelings-Iceberg.pdf.

## 5. Focus

- Van Durme, Yves, Nic Scoble-Williams, Kraig Eaton, Lauren Kirby, Michael Griffiths, David Mallon, John Forsythe, and Shannon Poynton. "Leading in a Boundaryless World." Deloitte. January 9, 2023. https://www2.deloitte.com/us/en/insights/focus/human-capital-trends/2023/human-capital-leadership-outlook.html.
- McKeown, Greg. *Essentialism: The Disciplined Pursuit of Less*. Crown Business, 2014.
- Quintenmenten. "The Return of Steve Jobs to Apple: A Remarkable Comeback Story." *Medium*. July 16, 2023. https://medium.com/@quintenmenten/the-return-of-steve-jobs-to-apple-a-remarkable-comeback-story-22cab5e6a71.
- Doerr, John. *Measure What Matters*. Portfolio Penguin, 2018.

## 6. Rhythm

- Duhigg, Charles. *The Power of Habit: Why We Do What We Do in Life and Business.* Random House Trade Paperbacks, 2014.

## 7. Cohesion

- Miami Heat 365, "Wade & LeBron Post Game Press Conference 2014 NBA Finals Game 05" [Video]. YouTube, June 15, 2014. https://www.youtube.com/watch?v=74eWzr4xIF4.
- Holmes, Baxter. "Michelin Restaurants and Fabulous Wines: Inside the Secret Team Dinners that Have Built the Spurs' Dynasty." *ESPN.* July 25, 2020. https://www.espn.com/nba/story/_/id/26524600/secret-team-dinners-built-spurs-dynasty.
- Duhigg, Charles. "What Google Learned from Its Quest to Build the Perfect Team." *The New York Times Magazine*, February 25, 2016. https://www.nytimes.com/2016/02/28/magazine/what-google-learned-from-its-quest-to-build-the-perfect-team.html.
- Edmondson, Amy. "Psychological Safety and Learning Behavior in Work Teams." *Administrative Science Quarterly*, Vol. 44, No. 2 (June 1999), pp. 350-383. https://www.jstor.org/stable/2666999?origin=JSTOR-pdf.
- Catmull, Ed. *Creativity, Inc: Overcoming the Unseen Forces That Stand in the Way of True Inspiration.* Random House, 2014.
- Covey, Stephen M.R. *The Speed of Trust: The One Thing That Changes Everything.* Free Press, 2006.
- Guthrie, Marisa. "Amy Poehler's Coming-of-Rage Story: Comedy's Subversive Star is Defining Her Own Feminism." *The Hollywood Reporter*. April 24, 2019. https://www.hollywoodreporter.com/movies/movie-features/amy-poehlers-ready-define-her-own-feminism-1204004/.

## 8. Momentum

- Skillman, Peter. "The Design Challenge (also called Spaghetti Tower)." *Medium*, April 14, 2019. https://medium.com/@peterskillman/the-design-challenge-also-called-spaghetti-tower-cda62685e15b.
- Schwartz, Barry. *The Paradox of Choice: Why More is Less*. Harper Perennial, 2005.
- Godin, Seth. *Linchpin: Are You Indispensable?* Portfolio, 2011.
- Mark, Gloria. *Attention Span: A Groundbreaking Way to Restore Balance, Happiness and Productivity*. Hanover Square Press, 2023.

## 9. Getting Started

- Clear, James. *Atomic Habits: An Easy & Proven Way to Build Good Habits & Break Bad Ones*. Avery, an imprint of Penguin Random House, 2018.

## 10. It's a Journey

- Turteltaub, Jon. *Cool Runnings* (Walt Disney Pictures, 1993), YouTube. https://www.youtube.com/watch?v=Rvi6fzyBNvQ.

# About 6 Levers

At 6 Levers, we help organizations unlock their full potential by focusing on the vital intersection of people and systems. Our proven framework empowers leaders to intentionally design their organizational operating system, fostering workplaces where both individuals and teams can thrive.

We offer a range of services including leadership development courses, executive coaching, strategic planning, and 6 Levers training and implementation. Each service is tailored to equip leaders with the skills to manage teams effectively while nurturing a culture of growth, accountability, and collaboration.

By aligning organizational structures with strategic goals, we help teams ensure that systems and processes are built for long-term success—all while keeping fundamental human needs at the core.

If you want to learn more about adopting the 6 Levers framework or if you are a consultant interested leveraging the 6 Levers framework in your practice, visit **www.6levers.co**